CHANGE NOT CHANGES

New Directions in
Religious Life and Priesthood

✝

by

Clement J. McNaspy, S.J.

PAULIST PRESS DEUS BOOKS

NEW YORK   GLEN ROCK   WESTMINSTER
TORONTO   AMSTERDAM

IMPRIMI POTEST:
John H. Edwards, S.J.
Provincial, New Orleans

NIHIL OBSTAT:
Very Rev. Msgr. William F. Hogan, S.T.D.
Censor Librorum

IMPRIMATUR:
✠ Thomas A. Boland, S.T.D.
Archbishop of Newark

January 26, 1968

The Nihil Obstat and Imprimatur are official declarations that
a book or pamphlet is free of doctrinal or moral error. No implication is contained therein that those who have granted the
Nihil Obstat and Imprimatur agree with the contents, opinions or
statements expressed.

Library of Congress
Catalog Card Number: 68-21455

Published by Paulist Press
Editorial Office: 304 W. 58th St., N. Y., N. Y. 10019
Business Office: Glen Rock, New Jersey 07452

Manufactured in the
United States of America
by Our Sunday Visitor Press

CHANGE

NOT CHANGES

Contents

For Auguste and Youree

Foreword

I AM ONE of those many "untrustworthy" American
Catholics over thirty who have survived Jesuit education. I recall it as a kaleidoscopic amalgam of for-
gotten Latin verbs, remembered debates, "jug," Duces
nominations and sodality meetings, bound together by
priests and scholastics, obedient men, who communicated
a collective martial certainty about religion and the Society which many adolescent contemporaries variously
envied or deplored.

The apologetic certainties of childhood and youth are
long gone. The present painful efforts of the American
Church to renew herself institutionally, efforts in which
we all participate, have been presaged for at least a
generation of private lay and clerical attempts to promote Christian unity rather than parochial manifest destiny. The Catholic Worker, the Liturgical Conference,
the Catholic Interracial Council—all, when in their infancy, generated the excitement of "belonging" to their
members. The European apostolic movements, Young
Christian Workers, Young Christian Students, gave our
generation of ex-servicemen a view of Christian life not
found in the American immigrant enclave. We were slow
to realize that the religious institutions upon which our
childhood certainties were built, were facing the same

internal challenges of authority, ontological relevance and community, as we were.

The seventy-one Jesuits who gathered at Santa Clara last summer for the marathon "think-in," so eloquently reported by Clement J. McNaspy, offer insights relevant for all Christians. Clement McNaspy, a comprehensivist "of a certain age," sees himself a bridge across the growing generational gap evidenced in discussions of Christian renewal, whether institutional or personal. In his person and in his writing, he exemplifies that graceful wit, eloquence and erudition which the world has come to expect of the Society, and which, hopefully, renewal will in no way mitigate.

As an artist and Jesuit "survivor," I am particularly delighted by the chapter on "Personal Development." The rights of self are placed in a context of realization rather than abnegation. The challenge of friendships, between men and between men and women, is explicated freshly and admirably. The claims of arationality are honored. As Father McNaspy aphoristically concludes, "our own effectiveness will be closely proportionate to our own affectiveness." The Santa Clara Conference pleads that human institutions be truly human.

ROBERT E. RAMBUSCH

I
Why
This Book?

To be perfectly frank, this first chapter was initially called "Preface." However, if I may judge by my own experience, people have a way of skipping over, or at best skimming over, prefaces, and there are some things I really want the reader not to miss. Hence the curious new title, intended to beguile the hasty.

For the reader must understand, in the first place, that this is no *summa* or compendium of spirituality; many core topics are not treated at all, or at best cursorily. Nor can it be said to be a trail blazer; the ideas contained in it can be found elsewhere, better expressed by better thinkers. Still less does the book pretend to be an official, semi-official or quasi-official interpretation of Jesuit or any other spirituality.

Why, then, this book? Because I am one of the many middle-aged priests or religious concerned about our current changes in priestly or religious life and dismayed over a communications or credibility gap between the generations. Not that I fancy myself in possession of some prophetic or dialogic mandate to close the gap. But I believe the problem is so acute that even a very imperfect effort may prove somewhat more helpful than none at all.

Being well past the half-century mark, I hope to be able to understand my peers' anxieties regarding the young and the future. Having been privileged to teach in a novitiate-seminary for a dozen years, and enjoying continued close contact with some hundred or more former students, I believe I have learned something from them. I have been lucky, too, while visiting seminaries and religious houses in all parts of this country and in Holland, Belgium, France, Mexico, Canada, Spain and the British Isles, to spend many hundreds of hours "picking the brains" of the young and their mentors. Retreats given to seminarians, brothers, sisters of several orders and congregations have helped keep me in touch with my juniors. I hope their efforts at communication have not been lost on me.

All of this does not, of course, qualify a person to be some sort of inter-generational bridge. He might merely turn out to be a straddler or worse. If at times younger readers may sniff odors of "paternalism," this may be simply the consequence of ineluctable age. If my contemporaries find my tone hopelessly naive, optimistic or conciliatory with regard to the young, I should like to reassure them that I believe firmly in the reality of sin, both original and otherwise, and that I do not suppose any generation, theirs or ours, to be totally emancipated from its effects. Young people may be as wanting as we were and are; but, if so, they are wanting in different ways.

Further, I am not so sanguine as to imagine that

either this book or a library of books can of themselves create dialogue, much less make dialogue fruitful. Our unexorcized instincts make it difficult to accept criticism, explicit or implied. Censorious as most of us tend to be toward any deviancy from our own preferred path, we are no less sensitive to disagreement. We who are older must avoid the Elder Brother syndrome (in the parable of the Prodigal Son). We should, I believe, also try to realize that when others express, extol or emphasize something new, they are not thereby condemning us or a style of spiritual life that has meant a great deal to us. Even if they are, we can be expected to show some of the serenity and perspective that are traditionally expected to go with accumulated years. For, uncomfortable as we may find it, change is here and we may as well face it gracefully. The reflections that follow (for they are no more than that) represent one person's effort—aided by many others' efforts, to be sure—to face change. Graceful or not, the effort is at least earnest.

Even before Vatican II sent out its summons for renewal and updating in religious and clerical life, Pope John's magic word *aggiornamento* had caught on. Everyone, or almost everyone, paid at least lip homage to the open-window attitude of the genial pope. Gestures, most of them merely token, were made toward *aggiornamento*, in a feverish or ill-defined spurt of loyalty. Some of the efforts suggested that *aggiornamento* meant simply overthrow; others led one to suspect that their authors had looked the word up in an ancient Italian dictionary, where its meaning was given as "adjournment"—as though we should go on waiting while decisions would be made in high places. As *aggiornamento* faded into a mere cliché, meaning whatever anyone wanted it to mean, cynics foretold that the whole impulse toward renewal would soon lapse into blandness.

But the Spirit was not to be quenched. Everywhere there sprung up conferences and institutes to study the problems of adaptation. Since the Council, too, more enlightened dioceses have begun to organize synods or senates, representative of young and old age groups. At official levels, religious congregations and orders have held chapters in line with the Council's insistence on deep rethinking. All of these are important, and some of them have faced issues with the courage and candor called for. But juridical bodies have a way of moving with extreme caution, addressing themselves to yesterday's crises, attempting a reconciliation of all viewpoints, especially the more conservative. They seldom project; their peculiar charism appears to be that of curbing other charisms from excess; their orientation is rather toward the past than toward the future.

Hence the need for different kinds of deliberative bodies, responsible but unofficial, free from the pressures of having to set down laws with their restrictive or minimalistic tone. Something in the nature of "brainstorming" or "free-wheeling" sessions, where fresh, new approaches can be taken; yet participated in by persons with enough experience not to be trapped in jargon or whirled off after gossamerlike will-o'-the-wisps; not mere bull sessions, but with some of the intense sincerity and liberation from constraint that mark the best of these.

The need was sensed, and thanks to initiative "from the ranks," other conferences and institutes began to be called. I have been privileged to participate in a number of them, especially those held at St. Mary's College, Kansas (the divinity school of St. Louis University, and

now located in St. Louis); at Weston College, Boston;
and most recently, the Santa Clara Conference (held at
the University of Santa Clara in California). Other
important ones at Alma College (California), Woodstock
College (Maryland) and Spring Hill College's Jesuit
House of Studies (Mobile, Alabama) have offered proceedings, the insights of which I have profited by. I have
also been present, as a speaker not a member, at the
Conference of Major Religious Superiors of Men, and
have had occasion to learn of problems faced by these
religious leaders in their quest for *aggiornamento*.

The present book is by no means a full summary of
all or even any of these conferences. If I draw heavily,
often without encumbering these pages with notes or
scholarly apparatus, on any or all of the conferences
mentioned, it is not as though I were somehow their
official or self-appointed interpreter. True, I have been
most impressed by the most recent and most comprehen-
sive of these conferences, that held at Santa Clara, August
6 to August 19, 1967. Since, consciously or not, I shall
be basing much of this book on the discussions, background papers and consensus positions of the Santa Clara
Conference (all of which are rather easily accessible on
request), it would be appropriate for me to describe the
make-up and procedures of the conference in some detail.
My personal assessment of the conference has already
appeared in *America* magazine for September 2, 1967.

Several years of preparation went into the Santa
Clara Conference. The participants included the eleven
Jesuit fathers provincial of the United States, eleven
scholastics chosen by their peers, and 48 priests selected
by a committee approved by the provincials; the novice
director of the Upper Canadian Province also partici-

pated. Every section of the country was equitably represented, as was the most diverse cross section of experience and age. The youngest, a scholastic, was only 23 years old (very young, as Jesuits go); the eldest was 62; most of the others were roughly within ten years of 45, which I estimate to be the median age. The participants were largely men with considerable contact with scholastics, both academically and spiritually. This was appropriate for a conference titled "On the Total Development of the Jesuit Priest." Since the conference dealt principally with the seminary course for priests, brothers were not represented officially, though very much of the deliberations dealt with religious life in the broadest terms. Thus, in this book I have tried to serve people involved in the religious life as well as diocesan seminarians and their mentors—future priests, younger sisters and brothers. For most of what was discussed at Santa Clara and at the other conferences which I have drawn from seems to me to be of more than narrow Jesuit interest. What we have in common is vastly more significant than our family differences.

At the risk of being insultingly clear, I wish to repeat that the present book is my own responsibility and in no sense shares the authority of any other person or group of persons. It would be unfair, then, for any of it to be used as ammunition in arguments, as though it were some sort of arsenal of authoritative pronouncements, a minor Denzinger or catechism of easy answers. It is simply one person's reflections on what he has experienced, heard or read during many years of dealing with young religious and seminarians. Unoriginal as it no doubt is, it is, I hope, not less personal. It is, thus, altogether tentative, and some will find it already hopelessly out of date. However, since the *aggiornamento* has hardly begun in certain dioceses and congregations, and in others is creeping along at a less than glacial pace, several friends have pressed me into writing the book anyway.

Indeed, without the insistent prodding and ongoing aid of Fr. John R. May (spiritual director at Jesuit House of Studies, Spring Hill, Mobile, Alabama), it would never have been thought of, much less completed. Other confreres, all from the same house of studies, who helped in many ways are John F. Armstrong, William G. Bachhuber, Joseph P. Barton, João Cabral de Monlevade, G. Robert Fecas, Eugene M. Geinzer, Alfred C. Kammer, Clyde H. LeBlanc, Emilio F. Moran, Edward W. Noel, Edward N. Pugh, Don R. Riso and Joseph B. Rochelle. Special thanks also to the rector of that community, Fr. Donald J. Martin, and to Frs. John Hein, John Stacer, S. Youree Watson and Hacker Fagot for advice and criticism, and to Fr. William Quiery of Jesuit Writers' Service, who saw the book into print.

To young and less young, hoping they will not judge me arrogant in so doing, I address the plea to be "more ready to put a good interpretation on another's statement than to condemn it as false" (*The Spiritual Exercises of St. Ignatius*, n. 22).

II
Change and
Continuity

I T IS HARD and has been hard for some time to engage
in conversation with older priests or religious without hearing something about how awful, or at least how
different, the younger generation of seminarians or religious seems to be. "Can you believe it?" a classmate asked
me in dismay, "these young scholastics want to have
coffee breaks with us; they want to do everything with
us; they want to be just like us!" He shook his head
anxiously, and the gesture betokened doomsday. "They
even call us by our first names," he shuddered in
honest exasperation.

Had my contemporary been present at any of the
conferences mentioned in the previous chapter, his distress might have proved apoplectic. The very opening of
the Santa Clara Conference consensus papers, for example, spoke of the "true movement of the Spirit, an
outpouring of *charismata* throughout the whole world,
not only on those officially commissioned to lead and
guide, but on the laity, on the young, on all" those at-

tempting to live lives of total Christian dedication. For these *charismata* push toward change, and change causes discomfort in those, old or young, who are satisfied with things the way they are.

That we need change, however, or that change is inevitable, seems incontrovertible. On the whole, what is being stridently argued over is the amount of change— how fast, how profound, how encompassing? It is not easy to realize that as recently as ten years ago Catholicism was presented as the great changeless fact. Many were even shocked when Pope John called Vatican II, and some in high places expressed amazement, since there was "really no need for a council." Today, some years after Vatican II, even the most reserved Catholic is accustomed to such changes as, say, the use of the vernacular at worship, and few advocate a return to the complexities and obscurities of preconciliar liturgy. Still, a vocal segment of our Catholics express concern over many specifics, as well as over what they feel is a dangerous process of things getting unstuck.

To many people, in fact, religion is synonymous with the great conservative force in society. Sad to say, much of history tends to corroborate this notion. Even historical Christianity, however revolutionary in its aspirations and initial impulse, has often been used by reactionary movements as a strong ally. Indeed, the Marxist criticism of Christianity, and not only the Marxist criticism, judges it to be the great obstacle to human progress. Yet, as Cardinal Newman pointed out in his *Essay on the Development of Christian Doctrine* (1878 edition), the Church is ever "germinating," "progressive," rich in "sudden and wonderful changes" and in "consolidations and adaptations." In a much quoted judgment Newman further states that "in a higher world it is otherwise, but here below to live is to change, and to be perfect is to have changed often." When Newman enunciated this insight it must have seemed very radical indeed; today, many would criticize it as too conservative for suggesting that we can ever be perfect here below, as though change would ever become unnecessary.

If, in the Church as a whole, change has stirred up reactionary movements that appear traumatic—such bizarre phenomena as the "Traditionalists," for example—it is hardly surprising to find tensions within more closely knit religious families or priestly institutions. For until recently, at least, the stress has been consistently placed on loyalty, loyalty to tradition, to the institute, to custom. Not that anyone supposes that a social organism, be it religious or secular, can exist apart from some sense of continuity with its past. It is unthinkable that anyone would, say, enter a religious institute unless he expected it to remain somehow recognizably itself.

Most vocations, I suppose, are personal in their human impulse: we want to identify with, to be like, someone we admire and who happens to belong to that particular community. Accordingly, we accept fundamentally the way of life that he accepted, even if we know little about it in detail. This means that, at least in broad principle, we accept some continuity, and when we pledge ourselves to a way of life we expect the way of life to go on being, if only in the most general sense, the same.

. Thus, the question of change and continuity in religious or priestly life is not one of absolute, total denial or acceptance on the part of young or old. Even the most disinclined to accept radical change grants that some change is inescapable, indeed requisite for survival; even the most radically oriented accepts the need or inevitability of some continuity. The poles of change and continuity are never, in the real order, absolutized. The tension, concretely, is one of reconciling and preserving both values, keeping either from becoming totalistic, preventing dialogue from breaking down altogether.

Fraternal Preamble

It was entirely appropriate, then, for the first consensus paper of the Santa Clara Conference (and much the same can be said of other conferences) to address itself explicitly to this tension. In what was titled "A Fraternal Preamble," the conference urgently recommended "two things above all to our fellow-members: first of all, that no matter how shocking changes may seem or however disturbing the apparently intransigent resistance to change may be, all exercise the highest charity of mutual tolerance, mutual forbearance and Christian patience. Indeed we ought positively to accept one another as persons and as Jesuits [read any other name or "fellow priests"], each with his own ideas, attitudes and practices, whether we agree with them or not.

"Secondly, we recognize that we are in a period of choice and creation like that of Ignatius and his early companions [read any other founder or revered spiritual innovator]. Like them, our future lies in specifying in our world the redemptive work of Christ. We urge that, community by community, we carry on the discernment of spirits to find God's will in our ministries and in the total development" of our young members.

Unimpeachable as are these two recommendations, they are about as difficult to carry through as any that might be imagined. The difficulty is not simply one of

crude egotism or self-righteousness, omnipresent as these
may be in some latent form. At least in theory we know
that we must be tolerant, that it is not ours to pass moral
judgments on others' deeds, accusing, assigning guilt.
Often as we may fail, in our more authentic moments
we recognize that such judgments amount to a usurpation
of divine prerogatives and are at best immodest if
not arrogant.

We Feel Threatened

A subtler problem is one of unacknowledged or un-
explicitized fear. We feel threatened by behavior that
seems to differ notably from the ideals we hold up to
ourselves. Many a priest or religious who has found certain practices or devotions, say, the rosary or stations,
helpful over long years, is appalled to see them ignored
or even overtly belittled by others. These others, in turn,
feel threatened by a vast impersonal structure of custom
or practice that appears unduly geared to past mentalities
and unresponsive to their personal, inmost needs. The
general distaste expressed, for example, by many young
religious toward specific forms of devotion—frequent
Benediction, perpetual novenas and the like—very often
is occasioned by a sense of phoniness or prefabrication.
How, they feel, can anyone really mean what he says
when he repeats certain high-flown acts of consecration
or ecstatic litanies, couched as they are in unreal roman-
tic or rococo rhetorics?

The resentment that many of us, I suspect, often felt
in the past but rarely dared express, is put into plain
words by today's younger religious or seminarians. Our
lack of outspokenness has been generously balanced by
what smacks of an excess of candor. For this generation

has grown up to value honesty above all things and to detest sham and fakery as the grossest, if not the greatest, of faults.

Young and Old

I should, perhaps, anticipate a difficulty that always arises when we talk of intergeneration or interage tension. As everyone realizes, however much it is overlooked in generalized talk, the tension is not precisely one of conflicting chronological groups. Many an elder person (one thinks spontaneously of Fr. John LaFarge, Cardinal Cardijn and a host of others) is as "open" to change at the age of 80 as he was at 20; others at 20 seem as psychically ossified, fixed and inflexible as their grandparents would be expected to be.

We all recognize this fact, though a human bent toward generalization and easy categorization keeps us from acting on our recognition. Perhaps prior to Christian tolerance, and accompanying it, is the effort not to put quick labels on others, not to call a person "conservative" because he is past 30, nor call him a "young Turk" or the equivalent because he is not. The sanctity of the individual person should extend far enough to keep him unshackled by labels. Hereafter in this book, if I use the terms "younger" and "older" in a generalized way, it is only for reasons of verbal economy; it would be difficult to restate the point of this paragraph at every turn.

Further, today's youth—once again I am keeping in mind the previous paragraph—has a particular dread of sins of omission. More than his elders, he feels it to be sinful when he is silent out of mere tact. Instead, to speak out, regardless of consequences to himself and sometimes to others, often becomes a supreme obligation in conscience. "Always be ready to speak your mind," William Blake put it some time ago, "and a base mind will avoid you."

An instance of this may be found in the *cause célèbre* that was the Hochhuth play, "The Deputy," when it burst upon the American stage a few years ago. Almost overnight, Pope Pius XII was toppled from his pedestal in the Christian imagination. The tens or hundreds of thousands he had saved from Nazi tyranny were overlooked. In the minds of many, all that stood out was that he had been "diplomatic" (a bad word in the vocabulary of the young) and had failed to deliver a thunderous attack on Hitler's villainy. Unmentioned was the probability that such a melodramatic gesture would have done more harm than good; instead, Pius was swiftly indicted as "safe," cautious, silent, compromising, equivocal, possibly even cowardly. All these are judged to be sins of omission.

Thus, when members of the older generation appeal to their juniors in the name of prudence or wider experience, the response, expressed or not, may be "So what?" The very term prudence has been denigrated to mean the unwillingness to take risks, the desire to "play it safe." Having been exposed, through the mass media and the paperback "explosion," to a constant bombardment of revisionist information about the past, even its heroes, the intelligent young person today is not easily impressed by appeals to the wisdom of superior age. He has read or heard too much Freud, Sartre, Brecht—often in journalistic rehashes or otherwise predigested, but far oftener than his elders suspect, in the original works—to accept easily what sound like the clichés of the past.

Words, Words, Words

Not that the young in turn, are emancipated from clichés of the recent past. In fact, it takes only a few minutes of listening to hear such phrases as "the sense of belonging," "self-actualization," "meaningful," "relevant," "self-identity," "fulfillment," or the like. These are lifted from books written by their elders, but to them they seem real, uncontrived, alive, not medieval or neolithic.

Such differences of vocabulary, as the history of slang testifies, have always been intercultural or intergenerational symbols. No less than changes in styles of clothing or hair setting, changes in styles of speech have long differentiated youth subcultures from the wider and more staid adult society. But to say this is not enough.

Anthropologists contrast youth situations in earlier cultures, notably in primitive societies, with our own. In the former, there appears hardly any discernible youth subculture; transition to full membership occurs smoothly, in an orderly traditional way, legitimized through rituals. Initiation brings one fully into society; one's status is accepted early, with full participation, despite deference to the tribe's senior members. Youthful energies are thus quickly incorporated into the wider society, which tends to absorb them easily, before they can be identified sharply or given a chance to become revolutionary. Such societies, for this and other reasons, tend to remain relatively changeless and static.

Hard To Be Young

In modern society, and increasingly in contemporary society, with its strongly economic-oriented value system, the young person goes through a prolonged marginal status. Today one can hardly hold a decent job without at least a college degree. Thus, until well into the twenties, the young person is kept in a state of dependence on his parents, whereas in other cultures he would by then have long been accepted as a full adult with a family and responsibilities of his own. The delay in our world comes about principally because of the youth's long non-productive status. As a no-longer-young neophyte, he finds his position ambivalent and deeply frustrating.

While the young person—for in many ways he is still young—is commonly far more intellectually sophisticated than his elders were at his age, he is incessantly and often rudely reminded of his economic dependence. He is not allowed to support himself; he has no defined role. He is, accordingly, resentful. He knows, of course, that a break will come, that discontinuity is in the very pattern of expectations. For once he gets out of college, he will be able to be somebody. He will then, presumably, settle down in the "decent life" of adulthood as unobtrusively as possible. Thereupon, economic and social pressures will prevent him from enjoying the status of a protesting rebel; deviancy from social norms and mores will not be allowed him. So, he senses, if he is ever going to rebel and change things at all, it must be now before it is too late.

In religious life the young person's position is roughly the same. Despite all his reading and the accumulation of vicarious experience, he is long kept in a childlike status (*in statu pupillari*). In most religious communities and seminaries, and often enough even after ordination for some years, there is no realistic or structured way for him to make a personal contribution that matters. During his previous education he has been trained to be rational and to criticize, as though to remold the very institutions that claim him and in which he now feels trapped. He is told to be responsible, but senses no chance to exercise real responsibility. He feels frustrated and protests: "Here, they tell us one thing, then do the opposite. How can we develop responsibility without some chance to exercise it?"

The same kind of contradiction or inconsistency he feels with regard to religious commitment. He hears protestations of poverty and sacrifice, while observing some of his elders conform to bourgeois mores. Now, he feels, is the time to change the world before he, too, enters into these bourgeois ways. He resonates to Reinhold Niebuhr's searing statement: "The kingdom of Christ becomes a luxury to those who can acquiesce in present injustice because they do not suffer from it." The last thing in the world he wants is to acquiesce.

Many Choices

Yet another source of dissent, expressed or not, is the very pluralism of modern society. In simpler, homogeneous cultures, youth was introduced into society ("socialized," as it is technically called) without much complication. The same would apply to religious institutes or seminaries some years ago. Today, however, the broad range of information available before and after he takes his first steps in religious life shows him that there is no single way of becoming a full person or of serving God and God's people. He enjoys multiple contacts with accumulated knowledge and speculation, and from them he learns possible alternatives to the training pattern his elders would have him accept.

No longer does learning, religious or otherwise, come down ready made from above, in a single channel of

indoctrination. The young person today has easy access
to widely diversified information and opinion; he can
quite readily read the same books as his mentors. Aware
of divergent interpretations of life, and specifically of
religious life, he finds it hard to be simply docile and
unselective; too many opposing opinions are available;
his very honesty makes it impossible to accept anything uncritically.

The danger at this point is that those of us who are
no longer young will be inclined to brush these problems aside as the same old thing, a case of history repeat-
ing itself. For be it granted that the generations have
always had difficulty communicating. Indeed, some of
the oldest human documents express this—whether in
Homer's lament that youth nowadays are no match for
his heroes, or among the earliest extant papyri, where
we find parents writing protective notes to young sons
away from home, or sons' replies to the effect that,
apart from money shortages, they were fine and quite
able to fend for themselves.

Not the Same Old Story

Such an explanation is too facile and fails to allow
for the decisive fact of our time: the escalation of change,
thanks to our multiple explosions—the "knowledge explosion," "communications explosion," "culture explosion," and others. Thus, though the situation is partly the
same as ever, it is much more not the same. Solutions
that worked passably well in the past cannot be expected
to work at all satisfactorily today. Granted that in our
dynamic Western civilization change has almost always
been a characteristic, the acceleration of change in the
past few decades is a totally new phenomenon, and the

young people of today have been brought up in a world very unlike that of previous generations.

Much less can we stand still and hope devoutly that this cultural momentum of change will somehow decelerate or come to a halt. Nor will the problems they generate be simply wished into abeyance. If anything, we can expect them to get worse before they get better. Further, this will be all the more acute unless we face up to them with an honesty that many of us find hard to muster.

"The human race has passed from a rather static conception of reality to a more dynamic, evolutionary one." This radical sentence comes, not from some underground subversive, but, surprising as it may appear to many, from the *Constitution on the Church in the Modern World*, of Vatican II (n. 5). The Constitution points to the vast changes in "this new stage in history." Indeed, it states that "we can already speak of a true social and cultural transformation, one which has repercussions on man's religious life as well" (n. 4).

The New Style of Man

We have already isolated some of these elements in this social and cultural transformation, and in the course of this book will discover others. Among the central insights of the new anthropology reflected in the documents of Vatican II seem to be these (as outlined by Fr. Gregory Baum, in *The Ecumenist*, March-April 1967):

1. Man is a listener, listening to someone, sensitive and open to others.

2. The personal structure of man is dialogic; he is involved in an unending dialogue which makes him to be who he is.

3. Man goes through a process of conversions, ever seeking to become more truly himself, yet ever responsive to a call that comes from beyond himself.

4. Man is in need of the community to become himself; this personalistic understanding is quite different from old-fashioned "individualism," for man becomes more truly himself through communion with others.

5. Man's life is constantly threatened by the situation of his life to become unfaithful to his divine destiny; the Gospel offers him sources of listening, dialogue, conversion and participation in community.

These and other aspects of man's self-understanding today must be reflected in human institutions. Otherwise the institutions frustrate man's truest aspirations rather than serve them, and deserve to be moribund. If the anthropology underlying the structure of a religious community or seminary is unrelated to the persons entering the institution, and for whom the institution exists, it is unlikely to prove a genuine means to Christ's service. Too often, today, we hear seminarians or religious who leave a seminary or a religious house say that it is not that the ideal presented is too high or too demanding, but that the institution seems geared to produce a kind of person they don't want to become. Even if such charges are sometimes exaggerated or used as convenient rationalizations, we must make sure that we do not shrug them off with rationalizations of our own. Rather, we must try to discern what the Spirit may be attempting to tell us through those young people who claim to have found us wanting.

Thus, the problem of change and continuity cannot be casually reduced to such facile formulations as "all this has happened before," "the pendulum will swing back as it always does," "young people today are spoiled by having things made too easy for them," "they are immature and should try to grow up," and the like. For, so far as I can see it, we are not simply facing an old situation revived or exacerbated.

While many of the factors entering modern man's self-appraisal may be familiar, either as something that is part of the ineluctable human condition or as something that has happened before, there remains something quite new in man's history: new emphases, new insights, new perspectives, and, above all, their totally new constellation. To try to see them with ancient instruments of vision would be like trying to probe the surface of Venus with Galileo's telescope.

Not Changes But Change

Our task, then, is not one of tacking on tiny changes to radically immobile structures. One religious congregation that I know (and the reader can surely add more), swiftly made a slight change in its garb, then settled down into new rigidity as though it had already had its *aggiornamento*. So it was that the latter condition really proved worse than the former, since any inspiration to real change had been quietly but forcefully put to rest. It is a sure instinct that makes serious young people so impatient and contemptuous with regard to tokenism. The imperative need is not merely for "changes" but for *change*. This implies the freedom to change whatever needs to be changed and as often and thoroughly as it may need to be changed.

What makes this so difficult, apart from fear or sloth, is the delicacy of distinguishing between the whims of a non-representative but vociferous pressure group and the true voice of the Spirit. Vatican II offers several general norms that will help here. "The appropriate renewal of religious life involves two simultaneous processes: (1) a continuous return to the sources of all Christian life and to the original inspiration behind a given community, and (2) an adjustment of the community to the changed conditions of the times." This means rethinking, in the light of the Gospel and according to the signs of the times (to use one of Pope John's favorite phrases). It will require, as the Council stated, "the suppression of outmoded regulations." Further, it will not take place "unless every member of a community cooperates." (*Decree on the Appropriate Renewal of the Religious Life*, nn. 2, 3 and 4)

Change As Theology Sees It

After looking at the problems of change and continuity from an anthropological or sociological viewpoint, we should examine them briefly in terms of theology. During the Santa Clara Conference, this particular treatment came during Session 26 (which may be found in Vol. 3, Part 2 of the Proceedings). The theological interpretation in the next few paragraphs is based rather closely on statements made at the conference by two eminent theologians, Frs. Joseph Wall and Bernard Cooke.

God's revelation to us is a self-disclosure. It is not something merely done once for all in the past, but must belong necessarily to the present moment, too. His primary revelation is the self-disclosure made in his Son, Jesus Christ. The fullness of this communication is achieved in Christ's resurrection, and all our contact with him is through the risen Christ. Christ reveals himself and his Father in the sending of the Holy Spirit. The

Spirit is sent to the Church; he is sent to each individual
person. The Spirit is sent to the whole body, but in a
special way—we may even say in a privileged way, so
long as the term is not misunderstood—to the Church's
hierarchy.

We must learn to discern the Spirit, as he touches
each of us personally, as he reaches us through the
Church—both the hierarchical and the charismatic
Church—and as he is at work in the whole world of men.
In the broadest sense, the Spirit's work is revelation, the
Gospel, God's Word to us. In the more restricted sense,
revelation or the Gospel is the distillation of the message
of the New Testament (and the Old Testament, too). It
is privileged, since it is the result of Christ's first communion with the Church. Since God does not lie, the
further revelation of the Spirit today must be consonant
with its beginning. Hence our constant recourse to Holy
Scripture; hence, too, the recent developments in religious life running parallel with modern scriptural studies.

Any further tradition—e.g., the tradition of our religious communities or the customary pattern of priestly
behavior and the life-style of priests or religious—must
be recognized as contingent. It must prove itself by its
consonance with the Gospel, which is normative, directive
and corrective. It must be checked by its consonance with
the Spirit-directed experience of our communities at any
given time of the Church's life, and with the understanding of Scripture.

Tradition and Traditions

Tradition, in this sense, is thus a living thing and
must change as it grows. True growth always involves
change, though not every change means true growth. The

two norms of change should be: (1) our growing awareness of what the Spirit is doing today and, (2) our
growing awareness of the Gospel. If we find something
in our "traditions" that is contrary to tradition (understood in terms of these two primary values), it must go.

When the Council urged religious to return to the
inspiration of their founders, this was a clear reminder
that the deeper tradition of the institute was what was
approved by the Church, not necessarily later "traditions." Any group has incumbent upon it the constant
re-examination of its own traditions and the testing of
them against the movement of the Spirit in today's world
and against the Gospel as the Spirit gives us to grasp it
at any moment of sacred history.

A great fact in the life of mankind that touches on
the life and thought of the Church is that we are moving
from a static, structured approach to one that is more
one of *process*. The stress on the Pilgrim Church or on
eschatology implies that things both are and are not; that
we are on the way, and not in a definitive state. In the
past we have stressed a blueprint sort of image of God's
will, as though, with no reference to our personal decisions, God predetermined the whole course of our lives
down to the tiniest detail.

Today, many if not most theologians see God's will
in entirely different terms. "God is sustaining creatively,"
states Fr. Bernard Cooke, "the process by which human
beings, with several options before them, and in many
cases options which are relatively neutral, any one of
which might be a good choice. They are the cutting-edge
of what you might call the Will of God. We human beings are meant to shape the development of history and
the development of evolution, even of the cosmos itself,

from this point onward." And if this is so of the cosmos in general, how much more so of the inner cosmos of the spiritual life.

It hardly needs pointing out that such an understanding of God's will does not make things easy. At least for many of us, it would be far more comfortable to imagine the ready-made blueprint as representing his true purpose for us. In our more supine moments we might prefer to have everything worked out in detail, communicated in dazzling and unmistakable clarity. Our task, then, would be quite simple—that of automatically performing certain operations and omitting others. Such a system would, no doubt, be uncomplicated, requiring only a passive acceptance on our part. It would fit neatly into a way of life requiring hardly any initiative, imagination or creativity, and, in fact, this is the way the concept of religious obedience has often been presented in the past.

However, the whole thrust of Vatican II, of contemporary theology, and, so far as we can discern, of the movement of the Holy Spirit in our time, points the other way. God has invited us, not to be mere objects of creation, passive clods with little of our own to do, but true subjects involved in his own creative work.

Church in Process

If this is evident with regard to the cosmos at large, and our own personal microcosm, how much more so when it comes to his greatest creative work, building up the body of Christ. One of the opening statements of Vatican II (at the beginning of the *Constitution on the Sacred Liturgy*) made it clear that the Council had as one of its primary aims "to adapt more suitably to the

needs of our own times those institutions which are subject to change." If any ecclesial institutions are subject
to change (and we know that all those of merely human
origin are so), it is plain that those which are of non-
hierarchical, charismatic origin must be preeminently
changeable. For their human origin (allowing, of course,
for divine grace) is evident, with a distinct history that
can be studied and verified.

Such, obviously, are religious orders, congregations
and institutes, no less than the whole recent system of
clerical training. These are not immutable parts of a
divinely fixed deposit, but represent the serious efforts
of dedicated people at a given moment of history as they
sought to discern God's Spirit.

Here, too, some tension is almost bound to arise between junior and senior members of a community or of
the clergy. The elders often sound as though they believed that they had discerned God's Spirit once for all;
as though he had left the Church with a completed message once upon a time, which message would be mediated
by them alone; or as though God had spoken definitively
and in full detail to their "Holy Founder," leaving nothing more to be discovered or revealed.

Younger members, in turn, often sound as if they too
had a monopoly on discernment, as though the Holy
Spirit had somehow been silent for all these years until
the enlightened present. While the elders stress God's
immutability (as though he had urged us to participate
in this) and the Church as a "spotless bride" and dogma
as utterly complete (however unintelligible or irrelevant-
sounding to another age), the young stress historical
process, fearing encapsulation, eager for understanding,
zealously honest about their failures.

Put as baldly as this, the tension between such opposed positions could never be resolved. Happily, what I have described is to an extent a caricature, so put for clarity's sake. The real hope, apart from a thunderbolt of divine illumination, is for serious, trustful, candid, loving dialogue. This involves more than talk about dialogue. It means something far more generous and unegotistical, too, than a series of simultaneous monologues, with each side simply talking and hearing only enough to find vulnerable spots whereon to score points. Dialogue is far from debate, farther still from crude argument. It presupposes a willingness really to listen.

They Don't Listen

One of the commonest complaints I hear from younger people is that many of their elders don't really listen. "He didn't hear a thing I was trying to say," many a young person agonizingly says. Dramatically portrayed in "Philadelphia, Here I Come," this has become a constant in recent literature. Not listening doesn't mean that others don't go through certain courtesies, the motions of listening, remaining politely still while the other person speaks. It means, rather, that the reply sharply suggests that nothing that has been said made any real difference to the flow of thought.

Erich Fromm, in his *Art of Loving* (p. 114), talks about the need of concentration in this situation: "To be concentrated in relation to others means primarily to be able to listen. Most people listen to others, or even give advice, without really listening. They do not take the other person's talk seriously, they do not take their own answers seriously either."

Older religious often complain, in turn, that younger

people shut them off, as though they were reckoned to be hopelessly "out of it." And, in fact, many younger people, unaware that superiors and elders are human, too, occasionally treat them with a bluntness that is interpreted as cruelty. Some of this is self-defense. The younger person, accustomed to long years of dependence before his entrance into novitiate or seminary, identifies his elders as some of "them"—the vague, diffuse, semi-anonymous "establishment," powerful enough to damage his precarious future.

From childhood on he has discovered that often his only self-protection lay in "turning them off," "shutting them out," in various subtle ways. This is understandable enough in childhood, but as the young person passes adolescence into young adulthood, he may be inclined to use the same self-protective tactic, to wear the same carapace, that worked earlier in life. Thus, he too may fail to listen and may make it harder for his elders to listen. Further, the young can at times be quite as doctrinaire and unyielding as anyone. The insight of e.e. cummings, "For whenever men are right they are not young," is a challenge not less to the chronologically young than to their seniors.

No Getting Back to Normal

Yet, when all has been said about the need for dialogue and openness, we must not forget that dialogue is geared to change. We would be exceedingly and dangerously naive were we to minimize the deep restlessness within the Church—and perhaps most notably within the clerical and religious-life sectors of the Church—as though they were some merely passing phenomenon. "When are things going to settle down to normal?" is a query heard every day. The answer, I believe, is that they never will settle down to normal, if by that one means a literal return to the past, and if by "settle down" one supposes that a few superficial changes are all that are needed before blissful changelessness is our lot. Even if non-change were desirable, there remains the truth of Chesterton's aphorism: "If you leave a thing alone you leave it to a torrent of change; a white post soon becomes a black post."

This paradox invites brief discussion. If we try to leave things alone in the religious and clerical life, we leave them to a torrent of change—not the organic type of change that bespeaks life, but that chaotic anti-organic proliferation that is cancer. For change there will be, whether we resist it or not.

But Chesterton's figure of the "white post" becoming black should not be taken too literally either. It might suggest that our aim is to change only enough to return to some mythical golden age of the past. True, the charismatic first moment of a religious foundation can supply a good deal of inspiration and guidance. Even there, we have to be careful to learn from this privileged moment what is lastingly pertinent and what is merely anachronistic and irrelevant to other ages. Tradition, as a great artist saw it, does not mean wearing your grandfather's hat.

Good St. Paphnutius

So it is that the right question for contemporary Paphnutians to ask is not "What did our Holy Father St. Paphnutius do?" but "What, were he living today in this totally different world, would he have the vision and courage to initiate?" For if St. Paphnutius attracted the great-souled companions of his time to do valiant service for Christ, he did it within the vision and perspective of that time, and not of some earlier day. He read the signs of his times. Indeed, he was a sign to his times. In the same way, we are to be signs to our times. Our function is to witness, to signify, to speak of Christ to today's world, more in our lives than in mere word. This can be done only if we are true persons—that is to say, persons of our time, since otherwise we are not real—sharing the self-understanding of contemporary humanity and truly participating in it.

But why the special note of urgency in today's summons for us to be signs? Because, as has often been pointed out, during a long period of defensiveness and self-isolation we have stood comparatively still. Like so many other Church institutions, we have hidden behind our protective bulwarks of custom or routine, while the rest of the world rushed along in an era of unparalleled acceleration. History tells us something of how and why this happened, and it would be ungenerous, unchristian and simplistic for us to measure out guilt to our predecessors.

If we are in a position to view things differently now, with sharper perspective, our responsibility is simply greater, just as the urgency is greater. "If," as Fr. Giles Milhaven expresses it, "it is important what every man does in *his* time and in *his* place, it becomes crucially important what certain men do at certain times and certain places. They are the ones finding themselves in a position to take the lead, to show the way, to make history of the people of God." Few if any of us can honestly say the summons is not addressed to us.

III
Commitment

IN ITS present use the word *commitment* marks one of the critical lines of difference between younger and older (in the sense described above) religious and priests. Again, much of the difference is rhetorical; certain terms or phrases strike younger persons as stale, tired, bloodless. How often it happens, once a younger person or an older takes the trouble to translate what he means into the vocabulary of the other person, that the other exclaims: "Oh, that's what you meant! Well, I hold the same thing."

But the underlying differences are not always so easily bridged over. Often they are far more than merely semantic, and are not reducible to a task in communications. For, though it is true enough that regardless of generation we are more alike than different, our psychic structures, our underpinnings, our unstated preconceptions and hidden premises are by no means identical. We commit a disservice to true mutual understanding if we gloss over this non-identity. Commitment is a theme that must not be blandly bypassed, or where differences may be gently blinked. For the differences are serious and deep; further they hit at the heart of one's whole vision of priesthood or religious life.

Traditionally, of course, when young and old are engaged in a joint enterprise, the young stress the value of the change factor, while the old stress the continuity factor. As we have noted earlier, this polarity is stronger today than ever, since the young have grown up in an era of accelerated change. They have, it appears to their elders, no anchorage points; they find no fixed points against which to gage change or its pace; they find their elders' nostalgic attitudes bewildering if not sick.

Today's young person, when he enters novitiate or seminary, confronts a problem not faced to anything like the same degree by his elders: the problem of multiple choice. So many options and opportunities are there, that he tends to be, if not indecisive, at least tentative about things. Afraid to tie himself to the wrong value or bet on the wrong horse, he is inclined to "keep his cool," not to go overboard. Long habits of critical appraisal make him inclined to withhold too easy assent; he has seen too many people commit themselves too quickly, only to turn back.

Change Is Natural

Still more, as Fr. John R. McCall observes, "the important thing is that he enters at a time when the Church and the order are both in the process of change." He has read a great deal, and knows what is going on. He is not surprised by change. Change is all he knows. Is there any other way? He is surprised, though, at the slow pace of change he discovers, and appalled at any reluctance to admit him into sharing in the program of change. In any case, he is not in awe; quietly or vocally, he is sizing things up.

Thus, even from the start, commitment represents by no means something cut and dried, as though all he had to do was measure up. He discovers no Platonic ideal, nor would he want one. Thanks to recent publicity given such cases, he is quite aware that many priests and religious have changed their minds, even after years of commitment or apparent commitment. He hears about permanent vows; yet he finds them often dispensed from. What is this commitment thing, anyway?

A little farther along the way, after first vows or after receiving minor or even major orders, he runs into disillusionment. This is, of course, more likely to be acute when his novitiate or seminary life has been a sheltered, unreal existence. If he is a religious and discovers that his group does not really work together, that many are simply "loners," he begins to question the whole system; for he became a religious precisely because he believed that he could work more effectively, give more effective witness within such a group.

Persons Not Personnel

Further, commitment may become even more difficult if he fails to find the satisfaction and achievement he reasonably anticipated. This may be because of the style of "training": not as a person but as part of a mass. His "formation" may have been Pavlovian, with a very limited range of responses to a limited range of situations, with no transfer value to other situations. He may never have been given the sense of really belonging and being part of the group. He may, instead, have been made to feel that what the institution wanted was *personnel*, not *persons.* He may have formed no deep personal friendships. He may have come to believe that his order was one, in the Voltairean formulation, where people came together without knowing one another, lived together without loving one another, died without mourning one another.

If all or any of this has been the case, commitment has come to seem nugatory if not meaningless. Even so, other problems—normal human problems, not explicitly religious ones—may have caught him unprepared, especially if the early years were too ivory-towerish. He knew, for example, that the commitment to celibacy involved considerable sacrifice. But while very young, he stressed rather its denial of sexual gratification; in the mid or later twenties, its sacrificial aspect moved more toward that of loneliness; later, in the thirties, the sense of having no children to pass life and its good things on to; still later, the feeling that perhaps he hasn't mattered to others, after all; he hasn't made a difference. This is only one of many illustrations of how commitment involves the unforeseen. Or even if it is foreseen, today's younger priest or religious finds it specially hard to evaluate, since so much of his previous learning has been based on experience and judged by experience. For pragmatism is more in his bones than it is in ours.

Institutionalism

So is personalism. Today's young person is, of course, not inclined to love institutions. Indeed, the adjective "institutional" is almost invariably a dirty word in his vocabulary. When his elders rhapsodize about "The Order," or "The Society," or even "The Church," his emotional response is quite different. While it would be unjust to say that he knows the price of everything and the value of nothing, he is more inclined to be cynical than his elders were when they were his age; not that he is less virtuous, simply more informed; he does very often distinguish between prices and values, and between rhetoric and reality, especially institutional rhetoric and reality.

His loyalties, then, are not directed toward structures or organizations, however exalted. He cannot commit himself to an impersonality. So it is that we hear that today's young person does not see a value in fidelity. The opposite may be closer to the truth. Fidelity he values, but it must be an honest fidelity. Further, it must be fidelity to a person or group of persons. Commitment must be personal——first, to the person of Christ; but this means commitment to Christ as present today, in the people of God. His service is the service of the people of God. And it may be within a group.

His service must be seen as relevant. His commitment is precisely a commitment to relevance. As a young priest, he wants to be more than an administrator or sacrament dispenser; rather, he aspires to be a witness, a John the Baptist, a voice, a pointer toward Christ. As a religious, he wants the witness of a group working together, a shared, communitarian witness; but community, to him, exists for the apostolate, for service.

Yet, as relevance changes in its specificity, he insists that means must change. The problem here may be one of reconciling the need for specialization and competency with the readiness to adapt to whatever the present or future will call for. But more seriously he may agonize over the gap between relevance and performance, whether in the Church at large, or in his own religious group.

Religious life has always stressed conversion as one of its core elements. Conversion is never done with, and it is as important to the community or group as a whole as it is to the individual. Conversion is, in fact, the same as ongoing growth in relevance. The fact that both words are now clichés must not allow us to forget that the reality underlying them is a matter of life and death.

Ours is a covenant religion. From our father in the faith, Abraham, through the Old Testament to Christ, we are a covenanted people. In baptism we enter the covenant; by religious vows (as Vatican II put it) we hand over our "entire lives to God's service in an act of special consecration deeply rooted in our baptismal consecration and which provides a fuller manifestation of it." (*Decree on the Appropriate Renewal of the Religious Life*, n. 5) Thus understood, religious vows are not simply a pledge of commitment, but are incorporated into our deepest baptismal fulfillment. Since obedience and poverty will be discussed in separate chapters, this may be the place to reflect on religious virginity.

Christian Celibacy

It is, of course, a biblical fact that man is created to have a companion. But, as Fr. Ladislas Örsy expressed it, "we live in the new age of the Spirit, the Helper. In this age God gives some men his own companionship in place of the human companionship of marriage. Thus, virginity is not so much a sacrifice of companionship as it is finding a companion and a friend in work who can fill my life." As Christian marriage is a sacrament symbolizing the love of Christ for his Church, Christian celibacy is a special form of fulfillment of the paschal mystery of baptism. By it we are called to relate in a specially intense way to the risen Christ.

If religious life is one of special witness, it is perhaps in virginity that the witness is most explicit and unambiguous. In Cardinal Suhard's famous words: "To be a witness means to create a mystery, to live in such a way that one's life would be inexplicable if God did not exist." Marriage is understandable even to those who do not believe in God, though they miss its higher meaning. But religious life is senseless without faith. "I witness to belief in God by putting my life on the line for it," as Fr. Felix Cardegna stated it. Consecrated celibacy is thus "the most striking witness to God in the world today." Little wonder that it is so troubling to the non-theistic world. It prophetically raises the God question. Its element of ruthless totality is disturbing to anyone disinclined to probe into the God-dimension of life.

Consecrated celibacy is thus not a negative or narcissistic attitude. If one kind of relationship is renounced, it is in order to open the way to deeper relationships with God, his people, his kingdom. If one precious love is given up, it is in favor of giving oneself in many ways to many others. Further, it is not in order to concentrate on self, nor even on some higher self-realization. Our spirit, if we are not to be simply egotists on a mythical higher plane, is that self-realization "should not be the central focus of our conscious concern" (in the words of Fr. Norris Clarke); it is rather our love for others in the spirit of the world-redemptive love of Christ. In virginity and throughout religious life, self-realization is achieved primarily through our apostolic love for others, and must be as much as possible subordinated to it in our conscious motivation. Like health, self-realization is best

brought about without being paid attention to; otherwise
we become narcissistic and hypochondriacal. Too much
mirror gazing is hardly healthy.

The special relevance of consecrated celibacy, as
young people of any age see it, is that they see persons
so consecrated not less loving, but more loving; not less
open to real warmth; not masking coldness under such
facile shibboleths as "charity for all." They see the truth
underlying Péguy's pungent aphorism about those people
who "fancy they love God because they love no one at
all." For Holy Scripture, especially the New Testament,
is no less incisive: how can we love God whom we do not
see, if we do not really love those human beings that we
do see? We eviscerate Christianity if we eviscerate love.

Human Commitment

Human commitment, as all things human, calls for
growth. Precisely because we are not automatons we cannot pretend that one gesture, one movement, one pro-
gramming is enough, in some mechanical once-for-all
way. As married couples need to continue to fall in love
and to grow in love, religious commitment needs to recognize human reality. It is a love affirmation, a saying
"yes" to God, which is initially made, but then continually deepened, explicated, expanded.

Thus (here I am quoting or paraphrasing certain
papers of the Santa Clara Conference) in the matter of
commitment, two main requirements should be present
in a candidate applying to the novitiate—or, analogously,
in a seminarian as he moves along toward Holy Orders.

First, his response to God. The candidate would either
actually desire to make this response in the religious life,
or else would want to so desire. Secondly, his experience

and maturity: there should be sufficient experience and maturity to predict reasonable growth and success in the religious life. His experience should have been the experience of normal life problems. Otherwise he might mistake these for more explicitly religious problems. A certain amount of demythologizing about life should enter this experience.

He should also have experienced a reasonable independence from his family and a consequent ability to be alone, since a measure of solitude is part of religious life and priesthood. He ought to have experienced some real achievement, and as a result have confidence in himself and his ability to do hard things. This also involves a mature sense of responsibility. He should have the quality of sociability needed to live with others and work for others effectively. He should be open to others, while maintaining personal convictions. He should be willing to be moved by a worthy ideal.

Before pronouncing first vows, a religious should be able to affirm that he wants to make a total gift to God. This is the case whether the first vows are temporary or permanent. For no one takes temporary vows of religion intending them to be only temporary. But this totality is not in a vacuum. The religious knows—at least in the periphery of his inner vision—that simple vows can be dispensed. He does not intend to have recourse to dispensation; he does not intend to be a religious only partly or for only a definite period of his life; he intends totality and permanence.

But he knows himself to some extent and he knows something about the religious life, and he may advert to the possibility of further self-knowledge or further knowledge of religious life leading him to believe that God's will may be specified elsewhere. If he is at all introspective, he may realize that it could happen that he would change so much that superiors or spiritual directors might advise him to leave the order or congregation, before ordination or before final vows. He does not intend this now; rather he intends the commitment to be forever. But he does not have to be able to prophesy with perfect assurance that it will never happen, before he can take vows now. In the same way, a habitual sinner does not have to foretell with perfect assurance that he will never sin again, in order to be truly repentant and receive the sacrament of Penance; repentance is not prophecy, nor is present total commitment prophecy.

What is more, in making his commitment the young religious is not envisioning an eremitical future; he makes it within the context of a particular community. It is thus a matter of justice as well as critical importance for this community to provide a context of authentic love and personalism. For if it does less than this it is not Christian at all.

The vows are often, in ascetical literature, compared to the sacrament of baptism, and the comparison doubtless has a certain validity. In the matter of commitment we know that baptism is not a one-sided transaction. In baptism the person commits himself to Christ and Christ's body, but so do Christ and the Church commit themselves to him. Religious life, which is a further expression of baptismal commitment, is not one-sided either in its commitment. The young person gives himself to God within the community, but the community, in turn, makes a commitment to him. But, in fact, it is God working in and through the community who gives the fulfillment of grace and response to the committed person.

IV
Community

ANOTHER word that enters just about every conversation about the future of religious life is *community*. It causes a number of semantic problems between the generations. It used to mean or suggest a fairly closed enclave, and to say that someone was a "good community man" implied that he stayed at home, related well to people at home and was very much involved in preparing community celebrations, feasts, entertainments, home projects. Today's younger religious uses the term somewhat differently.

It need hardly be said that the term *community* is used ambiguously in much writing about religious life. Some use it to mean an entire religious order, congregation or institute. Others take it in the sense of the single religious house.

The term has a further use among sociologists, and when people speak of a "sense of community" or "the need for community" they are often using it in a sociological sense. Even so, sociologists give it several meanings. It can refer, for example, more to a group based on sympathy among the members, who find the relationship a value in itself. Some call this by the German name *Gemeinschaft*, literally "community." Other social groups exist more as an instrument to attain some precise goal. For this they use another German word, *Gesellschaft*, literally "society."

Community in religious life has, I believe, something of both these meanings. Neither should be taken altogether alone, but both exist together in the type of polarity situation we note everywhere in writings about the spiritual life, and indeed in human life itself.

It would be easy, but far too simplistic, to say that the monastic idea of community is closer to the first of these poles, that it is an ideal based on community for the sake of living, without any special outside orientation. Its witness is that of the Christian life, lived fully, in microcosm. It is seen less in terms of outside work or the apostolate, as that term is commonly understood. I repeat, this is an oversimplified description of monasticism.

On the other hand, most religious institutions today, including those of ancient origin, tend to view religious life in terms of specific goal or work. Their thrust is sometimes described as more "functional" or "organic." Thus the type of community they create is in some ways more that of the second category, *Gesellschaft*. (A somewhat different use of these terms may be found in an excellent article on small communities in *Woodstock Letters*, summer, 1967, by Fr. Francis X. Shea. The article is an eloquent appeal for small communities. In the same issue is another article, "A Quest for Religious Community," by Fr. Edward F. Heenan, which anyone specially interested in the problem would do well to read, too.)

After going through a fair amount of the recent lit-

erature on community, I would be rash to suggest that
we are in possession of a coherent, complete theology of
community. In the meantime, we must do the best we can
toward working out solutions in the practical order.

Community: A Communion

One thing we can be sure of is that community in
religious life is a response made by a group to Christ's
call for us to be one as he and his Father are one. Thus,
community is a kind of communion, and the two terms
have more in common than their etymology. Religious
community is an expression of our love for one another
in response to the love that comes to us from the Father
through his Son, Jesus Christ. In any religious community, regardless of its specific apostolic goals, this bond
of Christian love is the source, strength, consequence of
community life, and community life is its symbol.

When the young person applies to join the community, he commonly knows rather little about its inner
working. The chances are he was attracted by some person belonging to the community, wanted to be like that
person, identified with him, and in a tentative, preliminary way decided to undertake the enterprise of becoming
something like him. This instinct, however unsure, helped
him to recognize the fact that community does play a
considerable role in the development of the person. Not
that he expected to be "turned into" a member of the
order in some mechanized way, as though it were simply
a matter of being shaped, or hewed, or formed, or
molded. Above all, if he aspired to offer himself to Christ
and Christ's work, it had to be *himself* he offered, not
some depersonalized zombie.

It may have taken the young religious some time to

discover that he became a real member of the order not
so much by measuring up to specific detailed patterns,
but through deep interpersonal relationships in community. The meaning and importance of this communal
relationship is clearly grasped by today's religious. For
(as the Santa Clara Conference worded it) "each member communicates the special sacrament of Christ's presence in himself and shares in the sacrament of the other."

This is not to deny the importance of the novitiate
experience itself, particularly (as we shall discuss in a
later chapter) when the novitiate is open, not detached
from reality, but a true initiation of the candidate into
the life of the order. One has to start somewhere. But the
on-going process of development is, I believe, more a
matter of personal interaction than of any amount of
instruction or exhortation delivered from above. Educa-
tional psychology has increasingly probed into the role
of the peer group and found it immensely influential. We
appear to be more affected by our fellows than by
authority figures, at least during the formative years
after infancy.

Not the Course of Studies

After a long study of the Jesuit program of studies,
Fr. James Albertson came up with the following conclusion, which I believe is no less applicable to other religious groups: "A Jesuit is distinctively Jesuit not because
of a particular course of study . . . but because of associ-
ation—over years, and on a level of deep, personal communication—with other Jesuits . . . The predominant,
determining and specifying influence is the complex of
personal encounters and sharings."

I quote this passage, which hopefully sums up his

thought, despite the apparent (or real) indelicacy of talking about one's own order. For there is so much mythology, I believe, about the presumed merits of "*the* Jesuit course of studies," that Fr. Albertson's demythologizing, if correct, deserves to be better known. It may also be of interest to note (as I did in my *America* article on the Santa Clara Conference) that Fr. Albertson's judgment was adopted almost literally in the consensus papers of that conference. To be sure, this does not carry any juridical weight, but it does show the thrust of the participants' thinking.

The particular *cachet, esprit, mystique* or whatever one wishes to call it, of a given order or congregation is thus more a matter of "oral tradition" than of any set of written rules or customs. The interpersonal relationships the members establish, the communication that goes on among them, the thoughts, feelings and imponderables that they share over a period of years, are what matter most in community development. When this is done for some time, a living, oral tradition arises, and this is profoundly educative. It goes without saying that this formation is on-going and cannot be predetermined to any number of years. It has no terminus. It evolves dynamically through the action of the Spirit within the community.

Community Discernment

This suggests another crucial role of community, that of assisting us to discern the Spirit directing and empowering apostolic work. Through discussion and mutual support, the members of a community both more readily find the will of God for their individual and collective apostolates, and more readily grow in the courage and generosity to follow that will. In this regard, a great aid is the community dialogue, especially for those communities that do not have government by chapter. Such a dialogue can take place at regular or intermittent times, with greater or less formality. But, more importantly, it should be a continuing climate within the community, if the community is to be both Christian and functional.

This on-going dialogue among the members of a community is, in a sense, no new discovery. The first generation of almost any religious institute can illuminate the fact. During this privileged generation, founder and companions lived the golden moments of inspiration, usually a collective sense of the Spirit. A sociological explanation of this charismatic moment may be seen in the fact that everyone had a personal stake in the venture. No one felt like a mere follower; rather, he was a contributor to the common enterprise of discerning God's will, then setting about to implement it. But the implementation itself was not institutionalized, much less mechanized. One realized that he mattered; accordingly, one put all of his personality into the task at hand.

It was not, of course, so easy for the next generation or the next to go on working with the same creativity. The ground floor had been set; from there on, the task seemed more one of continuing rather than of initiating. Hence a lapse in what some ascetical writers like to call the "first fervor." Mechanisms were set up as preservatives; institutionalization became the style of life; charisms seemed less frequent. Little wonder. Organization began to replace the sense of organism, authority was more highlighted than responsibility, the vertical took precedence over the horizontal, obedience became more esteemed than participation, the dynamic element seemed to yield to the static. This, of course, is not to suggest that there were no gains in the process. Improved structure, based on accumulated experience, led to a type of heightened functionalism; in some ways, the job was better done; fewer mistakes were made. These are no slight values, even if others were subordinated on the way.

No Slot-Fillers

The general mood of the Church today, expressed in Pope John's personal *charisma* and in Vatican II's de-emphasis on centralization and re-emphasis on the Church as the people of God rather than an institution, reflects the "signs of the times." For in an era that has witnessed the personal diminishment consequent upon totalitarian regimes, size is less a value than it once seemed. Where everything is computerized and automated, and efficiency taken for granted, one is less likely to make an idol of structure. Instead, smaller groupings, what sociologists call "primary communities," are now seen—sometimes through romantically rosy lenses—as the ideal. For in them the person is not dwarfed or swallowed up. One feels himself less a cog, less a slot-filler.

Thus, today the religious expects his community to resemble more that type of community which he finds in the Acts of the Apostles or the early annals of his order. True, he expects it to be functional, and is impatient of elements that strike him as dysfunctional. But he insists that it should be personal, "to embody and show forth a love that encompasses all the members." Authority (I am here following Fr. Robert O. Johann's analysis) must do this and must "offer itself wholeheartedly in the service of the members' union as a continuing catalyst of concord, a kind of focusing agent for the converging desires of the individual members to be each one for all the others as fruitfully and inclusively as possible."

Smaller Communities

This, it appears, can only take place when communities are reasonably small. Smallness offers greater opportunities for personal participation, for love to be shown in deed rather than in word, for genuinely communal discernment of spirits. Group sensitivity becomes possible, adding to the personal growth of each member. Anonymity, with its concomitant hazards, will hardly have any place, since each one does make a difference. The fears and tensions based on lack of understanding and failure of communication can be dispelled. Group prayer, either informal or liturgical, has a chance to become real rather than simply routine. Community apostolates can be promoted and reappraised with a freedom unknown to large, impersonal institutions. Religious poverty can become an effective reality, since each one knows that his attitude and behavior make a difference.

What can be done about those communities that cannot be subdivided and made smaller? First of all, are there such? The burden of proof is on those who affirm that they exist. In any case, *de facto* sub-communities can be allowed to come into existence, provided they are not simply the institutionalization of coteries or like-minded cliques. For a community, to be Christian and some sort of microcosm of the whole people of God, must reflect openness to diversity of tastes, competence, age, temperament. It should not be so homogeneous as to lose the values of diversity. For if we are to learn from each other, to "form" each other, to make a real contribution to mutual growth, each must contribute something the other hasn't got. If all is too smooth, rough edges will not be polished but allowed to become rougher. We need the give and take of pluralism if we are not to subside into faceless identity, or conversely into hopeless idiosyncrasy.

Further, a small community must never be allowed to splinter into the coexistence of solipsists. If it is simply a small dormitory where individuals develop no sense of belonging, it is no better than a large community, and may prove even less effectual. There must be sharing, communication, reciprocity. Otherwise, small or large, it will be not a community but a juxtaposition of hermitages. For non-hermits this is hardly a human style of life.

Large or small, however, the community must provide group awareness: who needs help? how can he be helped? how can he help me? Community, to be community, must be more than the sum of its parts. The experience of sensitivity groups, T-groups, and the like, demonstrates that in a true community there can be a new sense of group identity, which is by no means destructive of personal self-identity.

Indeed, if the group identity is not positively helpful toward personal self-identity, today's young religious wants nothing of it. For, (as Fr. John R. McCall analyzes it) "he is person-oriented, not task-oriented; he is more concerned with the Man who is a religious; we were more concerned with the Religious who was a man. . . . He must be first and foremost an individual personality and a person. He is worried sick about being and becoming a person." Nothing, not even the noblest task, must obliterate him or his personality.

Thus it is that in reconciling the two poles of community—the personal group and the task—we must not so stress the task as to seem to treat the persons as mere instruments. A group must intensify its own reality and self-identity; but, at the same time, it is there not simply for self-fulfillment but for self-giving. Ultimately, it looks not inward so much as outward. It is there to share in Christ's own mission, to form mankind into a community. But as Fr. Bernard Cooke puts it, "The Church itself as community will exist only insofar as it contains persons who in their own life have communally interiorized the mission which they bear as baptized persons and who communally share a vision of faith and the life of charity —and this is precisely what makes them a community." This suggests that our mission within community is to intensify Christian witness to one another; if this is done we can join in bearing more effectively and profoundly the presence of Christ to the world.

How these somewhat abstract reflections on community can actually be carried out will, obviously, vary somewhat from congregation to congregation, and even more widely from congregation to seminary. For the seminary's very purpose is to be transitory, to disappear, in favor of the young priest who will soon move into a very loosely structured community— that of his brother priests, often miles apart, and that of the parish community, which is so different from the type of community envisioned in this chapter. Yet, though in recent years various religious congregations have tended to be more and more alike, they still possess some individual stamp, often that of a specialized apostolic goal. Accordingly, the type of renewal needed will vary somewhat.

The Kingdom Coming

Yet, all are part of the Church and all share in the

eschatological character of Christian existence, which (in Fr. John Courtney Murray's words) "requires it to look resolutely to the future—to the coming-to-be of the kingdom." In one of his last published articles (*America*, December 3, 1966) Fr. Murray went on to describe the signs of the times that were fully recognized at Vatican II, at which he was an outstanding *peritus*. "The first (sign) is man's growing consciousness of his dignity as a person, which requires that he act on his own responsibility and therefore in freedom. The second is man's growing consciousness of community, of that being with others and for others which is revealed, for instance, in the phenomenon of 'socialization' in the sense of *Mater et Magistra*."

Thus, our religious communities, striving to live the Church's life most intensely, will accept their eschatological character as part of the pilgrim Church, in movement, never done with conversion, never perfect, never able to be dispensed from the need to change and the pain that flows from change. They will be willing to slough off whatever is destructive of the type of human dignity and maturity that correspond to the movement of the Spirit in our time.

The pomp and circumstance of another age, for example, which may have been part of the social self-understanding of the baroque period or the medieval, are disedifying in a society that values simplicity, directness, democracy, brotherhood. Is there any reason, to take one instance, why a religious superior today should occupy a place of honor in the dining room? It hardly seems Christlike to people of the present generation. Is there any excuse, today, for vestiges of social distinction— different community ranks or "grades"? Does it make sense, in communities dedicated to Christ and involved in serious Christian service, for some to enjoy privileges or emoluments based on age or titles, when Christ has given us such an opposite example, indeed an unequivocal command?

This is not to undermine obedience, as we shall see in another chapter. But Christian obedience must be as far removed as possible from mere power concepts or military symbols. True, the Christian life has always been referred to as a sort of warfare; but the enemy is precisely that of pride, egotism, pretension.

The Church's self-image today—as portrayed in almost every document of Vatican II, from the opening message to mankind—is that of one "born not to dominate but to serve." The constant example of this should be those vowed to serve the people of God, and most of all those placed in positions of leadership. Authority, as Fr. Murray states so clearly and develops in the article just quoted, stands "within the community, as a ministry to be performed in the service of the community. . . . It stirs the love of the charismatic members of the community for the community, to be shown in service of the community."

Christian Equality

Christian community (especially within religious life) supposes a type of equality which should not be less than that of the civic order. True, in community dialogue greater attention will be given the opinions of members who have merited it by service and experience. But even the youngest member is a member and is entitled to serious respect. His insights may, in fact, prove fresher and less trammelled than those of his elders; he is less inhibited by yesterday's formulas and may be more open to new initiatives. Anyone who has worked with young religious knows how much they have to contribute when they are taken seriously.

Community also presupposes and makes possible a mutuality of service. If the young have newness and vitality to offer, their elders—especially those elders who have never allowed mental sclerosis to set in—have a great deal to contribute, too. This is not merely in the area of cautionary "prudence," valuable as that may be at times. They can add an element of history, in line with the aphorism that those who forget the past are condemned to repeat it. True, history never repeats itself, as history itself teaches us, nor does religious history or the history of religious life. But the "oral tradition," provided it is not absolutely dichotomized into "old" and "new," but remains a long, existential continuum, is an enrichment that can hardly be replaced. If change is essential to the life of a community, continuity is what makes it go on being in some sense itself.

V
Personal
Development

THE VERY concept of development embraces both change and continuity: change, since that is what development is all about; continuity, since the person who is developing must maintain some identity, some permanence, all through the growth process. This is about as plain a truism as could be uttered. What this chapter will discuss is the change and continuity of the whole development process: how much religious life as we have known it contributes to real personal development, and how much it tends to thwart it. Hence, how much should be changed and how much should be permanent. Or, more accurately, how can change come about without loss of the values that make us what we are?

The young persons entering novitiates or seminaries today are, as we have seen, significantly different from those who entered yesterday, and it would be silly if not worse to pretend that they are not different. For one thing they have all lived with television since their infancy; for another, they learned of atomic power and jet air travel at their mother's knee. Furthermore, tomorrow's postulants will be different from today's. They will be affected by still different cultural influences. But we are more concerned here and now with the young persons now entering or having recently entered. If we manage to understand them and make it possible for them to develop effectively, they will be able to take care of the future.

Problems

In the past and at present some factors have worked against a priest's or a religious' self-discovery and proper self-esteem. For example, often their personal ideas and ideals have been isolated from those of the community. In some orders and seminaries, one phase of development has been totally insulated from another, as though we could train first the will, then the intellect, then the emotions—against all laws of psychic growth. Then, too, time is wasted filling out the calendar year, whether or not a person has already achieved the goals set for that period.

All of us who have reached a certain age could amplify these difficulties on the basis of our own experience or that of others who did or did not manage to survive. The fact that many did manage to survive, and to survive relatively unscathed, suggests that either the course of formation was not as bad as it seems in retrospect, or the human capacity of resilience and resistance to destructive forces is greater than a pessimist might believe.

Even so, this does not emancipate us from the duty to change those influences that need to be changed. For example, positive education for community dialogue can help solve the first difficulty; a better integration of courses should do something for the second; upward movement by demonstrated achievement can remedy any superstitious veneration for the calendar. Other problems can never be entirely eliminated, but steps can be taken to confront them honestly, realistically, even drastically.

Who Am I?

Each young religious or seminarian must realize that in order to give to others he must see and accept the person he himself is; that unless he accepts his limitations and potential he can grow no further. What is this "self" that he is? It is not something inside, a sort of "homunculus" or "ghost in the machine," as is sometimes described in antiquated psychology. Nor is it identifiable with the Freudian ego, the mediator between drives and environmental pressures. It is not even simply the soul. It is, rather, the psychosomatic composite, the unique, functional relationship of matter and spirit, the individual person, the "who" that I am. It never quite exists apart from awareness or consciousness; it is experience, process, the consciousness of being an identity, of being one-apart. (This tentative description is almost verbatim that of Fr. Carlo A. Weber and is based on the findings of modern psychology.)

The self grows as awareness grows. There are levels to self-awareness, some purely descriptive, some evaluative; finally there is the "dynamic level," when one reaches the elusive inner core of self which always remains something of a mystery. To become a real person one must develop a real self-concept. Little by little the child becomes a little person, identifying with significant figures in his life and thus developing self-esteem or self-hatred. The process of oscillating between dependence on others, which can be called "satellization," and independence from others, the knowledge that one can stand alone, is essential to growth. Fear of one's self and fear that the environment will be overwhelming is the most pervasive obstacle to self-development.

The young religious (and the same may be said, with distinctions, of the young seminarian) should realize that his task of attaining self-awareness and self-acceptance is very much more difficult alone; the whole community should be willing to try to help him with his personal self-discovery, integration and growth. Lack of openness —either on his side or on that of the community—will slow down or stop the process.

Contemporary literature can be a great aid to spiritual directors in their task of education to selfhood. The inadequacies of theory can often be met by a judicious use of novels, poems and plays which, at their best, offer a concrete image of man as he is. In the preface to *A Man for All Seasons*, Robert Bolt explains his interest in Thomas More, a "hero of selfhood," as an antidote to modern man's loss of a sense of self. For Bolt, More is "a man with an adamantine sense of his own self. He knew where he began and left off, what area of himself he could yield to the encroachments of his enemies, and what to the encroachments of those he loved. It was a substantial area in both cases, for he had a proper sense of fear and was a busy lover." This example may be a bit explicit and thus atypical; but literature can be a three-dimensional corrective of the rather flat image of man as the textbooks treat him.

Bad Novitiate Practices

In the novitiate or early stages of the seminary, conditioned learning has played a great part in the training program. Certain responses are considered particularly desirable and are strongly rewarded: docility, calculated humility, unquestioning conformity, and sometimes adjusting to the whim of superiors or directors. If the beginner shows these virtues he is rewarded by more or less subtle favors, a position of responsibility or some slight prestige (which appears very important in the rather closed world of the old-fashioned novitiate or seminary). There is, in many institutions, "too much conditioning, brain-washing and de-humanizing" in the training period, as many religious psychologists have pointed out. Granted that a certain amount of paternal protectiveness and satellization is inevitable in early years—whether of life or of religious life—if it is over-emphasized or too prolonged, the result is immaturity. Too often novice masters and others involved in seminary or religious training are not required to compete and thus can pontificate with answers to all matters. There is also the danger of an "elite" being formed early, based on flimsy judgments of virtue (notably those virtues that make the young person easy to handle); such an elite is often taken too seriously, consulted too readily about other people, who in turn feel left out and isolated from community or the centers of community power.

Care Not Custody

. It is temptingly easy and gratifying to try to mold younger persons into the image of one's own predilections by exercising superior status and authority. The effect on character is to arrest the development of good judgment and interfere with the growth of an authentic person. Superiors and directors should realize (as the

Santa Clara Conference worded it) that they have "not the *custody* of men's talents but the *care* of them" and that their "task is not to command but to co-ordinate their growth." What we hope will develop is no mere copy or replica, but a true person able to make mature Christian judgments for which he himself can be willing to stand responsible.

This type of formation or development allows for considerable diversity. Not all are called to follow the same path, even within the same religious institute or seminary. Once a person is judged apt for membership, the group ideals should be adapted as much as possible to him, rather than the individual be forced into a rigid mold or procrustean pattern. The young person should not be allowed to set up a plainly hopeless ideal, which will lead to frustration as he meets failure. His ideal should be one of *himself* at his best. For Christ's call went to him, not another, much less to some abstraction.

The young person should learn that pressures, tensions and setbacks are not unique to the religious life or priesthood, but are the common inheritance of mankind. He learns to recognize what problems are simply normal and part of life and which are in need of special spiritual attention. He realizes, too, that problems and tensions are needed for growth. He is able to accept them with good-humored equanimity, and indeed with a sense of humor, realizing that things will not always work out as he had planned. This does not emancipate him from using his right to be heard, much less from his responsibility to listen to others. At the same time, once he has expressed what he believes he should, he should be willing to abide by decisions of community or superior, without sulking or self-pity.

Anonymity

Irresponsibility arises out of a sense of anonymity. To be anonymous within a community, or to melt into the backbround of the community, means that one counts for little or nothing. One acts not through one's own decision-making power and one ceases to feel responsible for consequences. It becomes all too easy to fall into step, into the long black line, where one is not noticed. If one feels he is nothing he will probably act like a "nothing." The result will be spiritual withdrawal rather than a sense of involvement in the work of the community.

Today's young person, and hence today's young religious or seminarian, is perhaps not as likely to take refuge in anonymity. As a child he was not taught that his duty was to be "seen and not heard." He has participated in family discussions and decisions; he has developed a sense of belonging, almost from infancy; he has been told more about responsibility than about obedience; his parents were not remote authority figures, but companions with whom he expected and in turn gave more openness than was usual a generation or two ago. This is brought into religious life, and any lack of openness will be seen either as a rebuff to him, or as a personal failure on his part. Today's young religious is much more forthright, even blunt or tactless. Accordingly, today's superior or director must exercise more patience, understanding and personal humility.

This does not mean the abdication of authority or conviction, but a more prudent and human application of authority. It means that the superior must make every effort to understand the young member as an individual. Failure to respect his individuality because of a tendency to categorize will lead to a complete breakdown of communication.

Thus in discussing failures in responsibility, it is important for the superior to manifest his concern for this individual by trying to find out why *he* acts in such a way; whether, for example, the action is an indication of some deeper problem, rather than simply a violation of regulations.

Mutuality and openness on both sides will eliminate suspiciousness; they will help superiors to avoid an overhasty appraisal of younger persons as "disloyal" or "disobedient," when they are not so. The same mutuality and openness will help the younger not to suspect authorities of "tyranny" or "paternalism" whenever there is a disagreement. Only genuine openness and trust can eradicate suspicion.

Community as Supportive

We have discussed the advantages of smaller communities in building up a sense of community. But large or small, our communities must be both supportive and rich in interaction and help toward growth. Community meetings, geared to specific community problems and challenges, will give real scope for interaction; persons can deal with other persons as persons. For without both support and criticism no one can grow. These community meetings can help create a sense of truer responsibility, as members come to share. There is no reason for superiors to keep financial worries, for example, locked in their bosoms, even with the charitable motive of not wanting to worry others. Today's young religious are willing and even eager to share these worries. Further, their imaginativeness may well offer solutions not suspected by their elders. For years these young people have not been treated as children. If they are treated as children now, they will either rebel or (perhaps worse) regress.

Need for Friendship

Our view of friendship must be healthy. Friendship and its development cannot be programmed. All of us, to be full human beings, need real friendships from the beginning of life. Certain administrators and spiritual writers have so overemphasized and misinterpreted the perils of the "particular friendship," that younger people can begin to distrust themselves almost neurotically. Stress on psychological aberrations can often lead to a kind of fascination with the aberration feared.

The value and necessity of warm human relationships must be constantly and positively affirmed. If any cautions seem called for, it would seem more appropriate to leave this to spiritual directors, who, in respecting the individual's pattern of growth in experience, will treat the matter only to the degree necessary. At any rate, caution should never be expressed in such a way that one seems to be taking back what has been affirmed.

In point of fact, young people need deep interpersonal (and particular) relationships during their formative years. It should be evident that all true friendships are particular, for (to quote Fr. Weber again) "it is nonsense to suggest that a person is equally attracted to everyone." Obviously, too, every religious must have a personal concern for his fellow religious, even more than the general love he has for all men. But he will never love all of them in the same way. The use of the phrase "particular friendship" in its antiquated sense of "dangerous friendship" deserves a quiet and dignified—but immediate—burial. Friendships that narrow or frustrate the ideal of celibacy are another matter, and I will treat that below.

This need for normal, healthy friendship among all maturing people, whether seminarians, religious or lay, is often pointed out by modern psychologists. Vatican II, in the *Decree on Religious Life* (n. 12) is quite explicit on the point: "Above all, everyone should remember—superiors especially — that chastity has stronger safeguards in a community when true fraternal love thrives among its members."

Among other religious orders, the Society of Jesus in its most recent General Congregation also treats of friendship when treating of consecrated chastity. In a very affirmative way it points to the need of "genuine human love for men and true friendship," further indicating that chastity is "safeguarded by fraternal friendship and in turn flowers into it."

Celibacy and Sex

Particularly today, when there is so much public discussion of the pro's and con's of priestly celibacy, it is most important that clear instruction on the nature of love and sexuality be given to young seminarians and religious. Too great caution in this matter can be only self-defeating. For today's young person has grown up in a climate in which love and sexuality have been both over-romanticized in the mass media and debased in the popular cynicism promoted by such magazines as *Playboy;* Harvey Cox, in *The Secular City* (pp. 199-204), gives a very incisive treatment of the *Playboy* philosophy, showing it up as "the latest and slickest episode in man's continuing refusal to be fully human."

So it is that no young person can be immune to bewilderment induced by such extremes. If another generation's Jansenism tended to make a monster of healthy friendships, as though all friendship involved some veiled perversion, today's oscillation between cynicism and neo-romanticism makes it difficult to approach the subject with any serenity or clarity at all. It also makes the effort absolutely imperative. Outbursts of self-revelatory anguish doubtless make poignant and titillating book fare; and in fact they sell well. But for one's own life one needs an element of balance.

Instruction must be given in an atmosphere of total candor. Anything less would be worse than nothing. For one thing, no one entering the novitiate today comes from a hot-house background. Kinsey and Kinseyesque exposés have lurked in the periphery of his reading, often cheapened in sensationalized style, but never bowdlerized or understated. In almost every case, we may assume that novices are just about shock proof. The only thing that might, in fact, prove shocking is any form of dishonesty. They will trust only if their instructors are seen as trustworthy. Further, while a rather clinical approach is expected, and a fair amount of demythologizing is called for as a corrective to the prevalent neo-romanticism mentioned above, the instructors' attitudes must not be or seem overly defensive. Consecrated celibacy must never be presented as though it involved the denigration of married love, much less as a disguised escape from the responsibilities of marriage. Only those instructors who have themselves manifested a capacity for deep human relationships with members of both sexes are capable of imparting the kind of balanced instruction that this core aspect of the consecrated life demands.

No One Instructor

Moreover, can any single instructor presume to take on this task single-handed? To ask the question is to answer it. For no one can be such an expert as to be in control of all the facets of spiritual direction, even in the matter of love, celibacy and sexuality. Teams are called for. Obviously, where novitiates are far removed from each other or from academic centers it will be nearly impossible to have permanent teams of experts. Hence, the need for sharing resources. Qualified psychologists (lay, priests or religious) are available, and even if a community cannot afford to summon teams of psychologists, several communities can pool the money needed to secure their services. Further, spiritual directors should not only be professionally trained, but should be sure to attend institutes and seminars, at least every summer, so as not to get out of touch. It would be incredible if they had not read, for example, the books and articles (especially) included in the bibliography proposed at the end of this volume as a sort of irreducible minimum.

Man-Woman Friendships

Given the amount of discussion now going on with regard to friendships between seminarians or religious and young persons of the opposite sex, something must be said here. The discussion became somewhat dramatized by Maryknoll Fr. Eugene C. Kennedy's article, "A Quiet Catholic Question," in the January 28, 1967 issue of *America*. Following years of pastoral counseling, Fr. Kennedy finds that there are many "priests, brothers and sisters who feel deep human love in their lives"—love that he identifies as "healthy," "not a slightly retarded adolescent ardor," far from the "absorbing and self-satisfying crushes" that are often called "particular friendships," and which "does not distract people from work." He grants, of course, that he has encountered cases of "foolish virgins as well"—"largely narcissistic, they confuse posturing with a passion for life; they insist on instant intimacy, a kindergarten Christianity that can only play house with adult Christian values; that speaks but never really understands the language of personalism."

But these undeniable cases of naïveté and the risks that doubtless exist in the matter of such friendships should not blind us to real values, nor to the greater risks of an over-protective attitude. It should hardly be necessary to point out that total isolation from half of the human family is unreal, and that normal contacts with members of the other half should be part of religious or priestly life.

Perhaps the most natural context is that of apostolic projects, where, for example, seminarians or young brothers or sisters work within a group and with a group. The "shoulder-to-shoulder" relationship is more normal than the "face-to-face," though it should be obvious that the first involves some of the second; "modesty of the eyes" means something quite other than avoiding other persons' eyes. Within the group, with attention honestly focused on the good to be done, relationships develop as a result of shared work and interests. This is not to gainsay the fact that relationships will become personal and to that extent "particular." An amount and a degree of this will be good. Some emotional involvement may take place, but it should be expected that the young religious will be open enough with his spiritual director, and that the director will have the ability and patience to help him work through the situation. This will best be done, not only by a direct attack on the problem, but even more by growth in understanding, maturity and commitment.

Another normal situation for young man-woman contacts can be that offered by coeducational study. This will mean not only classroom meetings, but further cooperation in curricular and extra-curricular work. Common sense and good taste will suggest which phases of university life are inappropriate to young people who have made their commitment in religious life. But one can easily think of many that foster normal social contacts: glee clubs, service fraternities, dramatic societies and such. Again, if the young person is dedicated to his chosen way of life, it should not be necessary to list a series of prohibitions and permissions; something, indeed almost everything, should be left to his good judgment, since, again, the presumption is that he is perfectly open with his spiritual director, who can help him discern what spirit is of God and what is merely escapism or masked egotism.

There can be no question that this move away from over-protectiveness toward personal responsibility will result in the withdrawal of some from religious life or the seminary. Here, obviously, one risk should be weighed against another. For it is not a matter of whether to risk or not to risk. The rather traditional protective approach has often led to delayed maturity, as though one could mature by simply waiting; for maturity cannot be equated with mere age. Anyone who has kept in touch with the products of seminaries or religious institutions knows how many persons (even if statistics are hard to come by) have passed ordination or reached early middle age sheltered from this side of reality only to "leap over the wall" at the first encounter with heterosexual friendship. Age and years "in religion" proved no bulwark whatever. "Hot-house maturity" has never been effective maturity.

Thus, the policy of over-security, as we know from experience, simply leads to delayed maturity, not to maturity. Some exposure to meaningful man-woman relationships at an early age is the only way to build up a realistic set of attitudes, as removed from romanticism as from cynicism. (I would like to say such relationships "build up a certain tolerance, immunity or resistance" to infatuation, except that it makes the whole growth process sound as though one were merely avoiding germs or disease; however, with that proviso, the medical metaphors may be apt enough.)

Granted that some young persons will discover that their commitment to celibacy was not as well-grounded or mature as they first thought. They will, accordingly, either grow in this, or in some cases conclude that they had made a mistake and will leave seminary or religious institute. This will happen particularly if they entered before having normal heterosexual social contacts. Again, though, it is far better for them and for the religious group if this discovery is made early, before ordination or solemn vows, and in any case before they are permanently ill equipped for life either under religious vows or under marriage vows.

The Risks

We may grant—indeed we should be perfectly clear in admitting—that a number of risks may follow upon this more open approach. Some mistakes of judgment will be made; some will be misguided, particularly if their rapport with superiors or spiritual directors is not genuine. However, a few lesser mistakes are vastly preferable to greater mistakes and the calamity of a later discovery that one had missed one's vocation altogether.

Something obviously has to be said about manifestations of affection. However, here as in other areas of human relationship it is extremely difficult to generalize accurately. Expressions of affection are a normal sign of mature love and are by no means confined to the man-woman relationship that leads to marriage. Neither are they limited to heterosexual relationships. Human affection is most generally and genuinely expressed by the eyes, by words, by gestures. Where human love is concerned, much more is frequently conveyed by facial expressions or tone of voice than by words. It seems important to stress again that the normal posture of those who love one another is side-by-side, facing outward toward the world, rather than face-to-face which possibly suggests a turning away from the world to rest in a kind of need-fulfillment.

It is clear that expression of affection for those vowed to celibacy cannot lead to genital expression. Here the word "genital" is used advisedly and precisely (it was the term used at this point by the Santa Clara Conference and its participating psychologists and spiritual directors); it is used rather than such vague terms as "sexual" or "physical." "Genital" of course, refers not only to physical union, but also to gestures, actions or attitudes that normally lead toward sexual intercourse. There is here another reason for perfect candor with one's spiritual director. In the matter of sexuality, no two people are exactly alike. While mature persons have instincts to guide them here—instincts aided by grace, to be sure—younger persons are more in need of the wise friend, the confessor, the counsellor.

Although in the minds of some, "sexual" can convey the same meaning as "genital" it more often confuses the issue and sounds as if it were possible to deny sexuality in the human relationship. In the broadest and the scientifically accurate sense, all human love has a sexual (though not a genital) implication, since the individuals enter as men or women, as total persons. The word "sexual" has to do with the individual's total psychological makeup. The word "physical" again says too much, because it may imply to some that all physical contact is out of the question. Obviously, rationalization is possible in this area; hence the serious need again for great candor with one's spiritual director.

Absorption and Self-Gratification

A more subtle risk, and perhaps more important for that reason, is that of a total emotional absorption which, instead of leading to maturity, impedes psychological and spiritual growth. The signs of this are somewhat more difficult to discern, and here especially openness between the young person and his spiritual director is necessary. In a problematic friendship, it will help a great deal if the spiritual director is in contact with both persons. A degree of candor, too, between both young persons can be a great help. For if the friendship is true, neither party will want to cause a loss of peace to the other.

Perhaps the subtlest and most serious danger is that

of one person using another for gratification of unacknowledged psychological needs. Respect for the other, for his or her commitment or vows, for his or her identity as a person should be foremost. For if one plunges into the world of warm interpersonal friendships merely for one's own benefit, the whole value is frustrated. Self development, like health, is not achieved by making a fetish of it. The good of the other, not self-aggrandizement, must be the foremost aim; otherwise the consequence will be, not maturity, but prolonged immaturity if not regression.

It would be counterproductive if the new freedom of religious students and seminarians to relate (in normal social circumstances) to lay students of their own age should prevent or distract them from establishing deep personal relationships with members of their own special communities. These mature relationships with members of their own communities are absolutely necessary if they are to identify with the men (or women) that they will be working closely with later on, and for the ultimate effectiveness of their apostolic teamwork.

I am, in a way, sorry to have to spend so many pages on the question of friendship and thus possibly magnify it beyond proportion. Indeed, the problem is how to say the right amount: too little, and no help is given; too much, and a resultant distortion. However, since the matter has been deemed worth studying at recent conferences which I have attended, I felt that a good deal of clarification would be useful. On the other hand, those engaged in the arduous and mercurial task of assisting in the personal development of young religious and seminarians will recognize that only an outline of a new approach is offered here. Their task is one of constant discernment

which becomes possible only if openness between them
and their younger brethren is both total and two-way.

Mental Health

Vatican II put great stress on maturity and mental
health in religious life, and the same themes have been
developed in subsequent congregations and chapters of
several religious orders. I hope to be forgiven if I allude
once again to that of my own order, since I am more
familiar with it. Repeatedly it stresses the importance of
"maturity," "the genuine integration of human values,"
"unification of the whole personality," "sense of responsibility," "true dialogue with openness and candor,"
changes in "our whole training in spirituality," finding
the inspiration of the Holy Spirit "through subjects as
well as through superiors," and the like. Our recent Congregation insisted on "sufficient human maturity" in
candidates, recommending that since "in our own time
affective maturity has become more difficult" for the
young, that more consultation be made of "men skilled
in psychology" and that the time of admission be post-
poned when it seems advisable; and that meanwhile
applicants be helped "toward obtaining maturity." While
it is plain that this insistence is far wider in application
than simply the matter of personal development through
affective maturity, the latter is one of the most pressing
of contemporary problems. The Congregation even expli-
citizes as precious the "ever more perfect love of friendship" found in "that mature, simple, anxiety-free dealing
with the men and women with whom and for whom we
exercise our ministry for the building up of the body
of Christ."

The Lord has often chosen for his celibate apostles

people who tend to fall in love and who probably will find themselves more or less in love with someone a half dozen times in their lives: the curious, affectionate, sensitive, warm-hearted, integrally masculine or feminine people who would have done well in married life. A dozen saints come immediately to mind as examples of just such people. Wise religious leaders—and many a leader in secular enterprises too—will scour the earth to recruit men and women who have these qualities preeminently, since such personalities have always been the most successful in every kind of work. These rich resources of affectivity and devotion are not something to combat and fight against. Rather they are to be gratefully, continuously and creatively directed toward the service of God and his world.

This positive approach to the whole area of psychological development is, of course, hard to achieve. Very much of the ascetical literature of the recent past overstressed fears and perils. Some of this, in fact, led to the type of fantasizing so effectively and gruesomely portrayed in the traditional paintings of "The Temptations of St. Anthony" (by Bosch and other masters). The false, glamorized, romanticized images of women led to a dreamlike world of phantasmagoria quite unrelated to real life. Perhaps anxiety was an inevitable ingredient of the life of early fathers of the desert, training to be hermits in total solitude. If so, it was a wise intuition of St. Benedict not to allow young monks to become hermits at all, and indeed to allow the eremetical life only to those who had achieved maturity after long life in common.

For if man is a social animal, Christian man is no less so. Rather more so. The Christian relates to God in society, as a true person in the people of God. His ideal is, of course, love rather than a stoic self-sufficiency. He goes to God in community. His formation in the Christian community is achieved neither as a solipsist nor as a gregarious conformist. Community, as we have seen, is not the same as military machinery, much less an ant-hill uniformity. Nor can a religious community be merely a barracks of coexisting celibates loving no one. On the contrary, it exists to provide a corporate witness of more not less Christian love.

Christ walked as incarnate love in the lives of men and women. He loved them, and not merely in some abstract way. His friends were personal friends and were attracted by him. In him divine love was channeled through human love. He cured persons by touching them. Schillebeeckx (on pages 15-16 of *Christ the Sacrament of the Encounter with God*) illustrates how the Christian concept of sacramentality goes with that of bodiliness. For, as Pascal said long ago, "Man is neither angel nor beast, and whoever tries to play the angel plays the beast." Angelism is no less a misreading of the New Testament than any other heresy, even if it has not been explicitly so-called in any ecumenical council.

The Christian must learn not to fear or suspect his emotional life. His feelings are, by and large, the best source of information about himself, because (as Fr. Carlo Weber explains) "they indicate his total, personal reaction to his life experiences." Any hygiene of emotion suggests, further, that man must first know, accept and appreciate the meaning of his emotions before he can control them. It hardly needs saying that this involves considerable openness with one's directors, as well as considerable openness to one's inner self. For growth into maturity is not a solitary activity.

The expression of feeling will not take cheap short cuts or easy ways out. Indeed, the "love of restraint" (as psychiatrists have called it) is indispensable in any relationship, whether in married life or in that of religious celibacy. It involves enormous respect for the other, for his needs, his sensitivity. The greater freedom one possesses, the greater one's opportunity to respect the other's freedom and the greater need for this. For our task as Christians is to be more for others, and self-gratification should be the farthest thing from our real intentions. Here the need for discernment is not so much to become aware of danger, but to reap the benefits of self-giving. More accurately, one concentrates more on the giving than on the self, and much more on the giving than on any benefits to be derived.

One of the fine steps in the renewal initiated by Vatican II in the lives of diocesan priests has been an increased sense of brotherhood, of the wider community of priests who do not live "in community." "All priests are united among themselves in an intimate sacramental brotherhood," states the *Decree on the Priestly Life*. They are invited to work with one another, to provide mutual help and to achieve "some kind or other of community life," precisely for mutual assistance in spiritual development.

Seminaries, too, are to be geared "to the age of the students, so that they can gradually learn to govern themselves, to make wide use of their freedom, to act on their own initiative and energetically, and can know how to work along with their confreres and lay people as well" (*Decree on Priestly Formation*, n. 11). The many formal and informal groups and associations of priests that have sprung up since the Council are in line with its directives and in fulfillment of the deep need for mutual support that benefits Christians. For priests are not hermits, any more than religious are.

The development of the Christian person is, in its psychological dimension, the development of the person. For it is a truism that nature and grace come from the same God and are interrelated within the same self. If to be a Christian is not to be less a person, but a person with a fuller reality, our aim in psychological development is in no way to diminish supernatural values.

The self, as we have seen, becomes the self as awareness grows and as awareness of others grows. Do you recall that key scene in the film "David and Lisa"? Only as Lisa asks of David, the person she values above all, "David, David, look at me; look at me and tell me: whom do you see?" and David's all-important reply reveals the need for self-discovery. "I see a girl," he says, "a pearl of a girl." It is much the same with all of us, as we become fully persons through each other, through love and friendship. And it may be that our own effectiveness will be closely proportionate to our affectiveness.

VI
Spiritual
Direction

"THERE IS a tree that's got a real problem," said the midwesterner in the parable. "It's too tall. It hasn't got nearly enough leaves. And it doesn't produce any maple syrup." The parable was made up by Fr. Justin Kelly, during the Santa Clara Conference, after seeing his first live palm tree. For some people, spiritual direction seems to mean trying to make everyone "standard" —turning spiritual palm trees into maples, or whatever tree one judged all trees should be like.

If anything said in the chapter on psychological development was true, it should be transparent that such a notion of spiritual direction has got to go. For the spiritual and the psychological are not airtight compartments ("grace builds on nature," as the traditional adage put it), and if we pretend they are, we risk falling into old-fashioned dualism that has nothing to do with Christianity. Spiritual direction, whatever it is, must respect the development of the person being directed. It must never try to turn spiritual palm trees into maples or any other tree, but simply make it possible for the palm tree to be the finest palm tree it can be.

Plainly, if a religious institute is designed only for maple trees, oaks, elms, pines or cypresses, the aspiring young palm may not belong. But even within the single Order of Palms surely there must be room for the 15 or more varieties of palms native to the United States, and quite possibly for the 200 or so species that have found it possible to grow here. A religious order has more in common with a rich, diversified grove or an opulent botanical garden charged with pied beauty and the grandeur of God. Even the most functional order can hardly be likened to a stiff lane of almost identical palms lining a suburban boulevard. In nature, and presumably in grace, uniformity seems to have little place if any.

Spiritual direction has nothing in common with military training as it has been known in the world's armies since the days of Prussian or Napoleonic conquests. The saint whose aegis is often invoked in favor of the soldier concept of religious life—Ignatius Loyola—envisioned, not faceless, cipherlike cogs in a military machine, but the intensely personal knight doing battle against the powers of evil. If he and other religious initiators did, with no little reluctance, come to grant the need of structures and some organization, it was not in order to diminish, much less obliterate, human personality but to heighten its effectiveness within community.

The previous chapter has already summarized some of the needs in personal development. Young persons find it hard to believe in themselves, even to face themselves. Often what appears to be pride or cockiness is only a defensive mask covering their poor image of self. Especially when they plunged into seminary or religious life

at a psychologically or emotionally extreme young age
they are beset with fears: of being hollow, empty, with
nothing to offer to others, irrelevant, ineffective, unable
to reach people.

More than anything else they dread the possibility of
doing nothing significant with their lives. They sometimes feel alienated, not recognizing that there may be
good reasons why even a successful person can sometimes
feel empty. They may have trouble distinguishing between loneliness as a creative part of human experience,
opening man to the unknown, and self-dejection, which
is not real loneliness but fear. Some may be naive enough
to think that there exists a happy state known as self-
fulfillment that insures instant happiness, and haven't yet
learned to struggle to make their lives count for something by serving others. They may not yet realize that
problems they experience now are not precisely religious
ones, but human ones, the common lot of mankind. All
of this adds up to the necessity of great sensitivity on
the part of spiritual directors, who must grasp the delicacy of the situation and be aware of individual, personal needs.

Spiriual Midwifery

What, then, is spiritual direction to mean? Obviously
it cannot be a substitute for life. No spiritual director,
least of all the Lord himself, simply directs. At most his
role is what Socrates would call maieutic—a sort of spiritual midwifery. He is neither spiritual father nor mother
to his charges. "Only one is your Father, in heaven." The
spiritual obstetrician assists, counsels, identifies and helps
remove some obstacles; but little else. Nor is this meta-
phor satisfactory. It exaggerates the role of the spiritual

director, as though the young person were relatively helpless and newborn. Such is not the case. When he enters religious life he already has a developing personality and spirituality, and this must be respected and allowed to go on developing.

Spiritual direction means assisting the person to become a listener to God's call and to learn how to respond, how to be responsible, how to discern. Urs von Balthasar has something pertinent on this: "The man obedient to his mission fulfills his own being, although he could never find this archetype and ideal of himself by penetrating to the deepest center of his nature. . . . Simon, fisherman, before his meeting with Christ, however thoroughly he might have searched within himself, could not possibly have found a trace of 'Peter.' Yet the form 'Peter,' the particular mission reserved for him alone, which till then lay hid in the secret of Christ's soul and, at the moment of this encounter, was delivered over to him sternly and imperatively—was to be the fulfillment of all that in Simon would have sought vainly for a form ultimately valid in the eyes of God and for eternity." (*Prayer*, p. 49) Christ did not give Peter simply a new vision, but a vision consonant with what he really could be.

If we may extrapolate from several tables of the *Survey of American Jesuits* (cf. chapter IX), it seems evident that young religious and seminarians today place a great deal of importance on spiritual direction. Table 40, on the meaningfulness of conferences with spiritual directors, shows that among those in the first five years following novitiate, between 60 and 70 per cent rate the meaningfulness as "quite a bit" or "very much so," while from 20 to 25 per cent rate it as "more or less," and only a small percentage find it "hardly at all" or "not at all."

The older men, as would be expected, place less importance on spiritual direction. My surmise is that this is for two reasons: as one grows in maturity one needs less direction from a director, since he gains more from the wisdom of his friends; and at least many of the more recently appointed directors have been better selected and prepared, and may thus be expected to do a better job. Table 137 ("What factors do you think would contribute most to the greater effectiveness of our apostolic work as a whole?") was directed to priests and resulted in an overwhelming indication that spiritual training came first; this table allowed the respondents to choose whatever values they preferred; thus the preference is not only for spiritual training over one or other single value, but over any and all that might be thought of.

More Than Ever Today

The need for competent spiritual direction is probably more sharply felt today than in the past. For today, especially following Vatican II, there is great stress on the values in the lay vocation, and a certain amount of exposé-type autobiographical writing has tended to call religious and priestly vocations into question. Even an improved and open type of novitiate cannot anticipate every problem; much less can solutions be legislated.

Today's increased freedom means more sensitive, skilled, personal direction. Further, many young people enter novitiate or seminary without ever having been really "laymen." Thus, they may simplistically suppose that the life of the adult layman presents no spiritual problems—the old myth of greener pastures. Still more, the proliferation of books on spirituality or popular theology makes some direction imperative, if only as a remedy against muddleheadedness.

What, then, should a spiritual director be? He should be a person with both technical competence and personal effectiveness. He should, of course, know his limits and be prepared to say frequently "I don't know." For no one can know all the answers. He will also be a person ready to consult others, especially others in allied disciplines like psychology. He will also make generous use of referral, since he should know enough psychology to know what he is not qualified to handle himself. He will go to spiritual institutes and attend summer sessions in direction and counseling as often as possible.

He will himself try to grow in the understanding of his role. He will have the greatest respect for individuals, not attempting to mold them into his own image and likeness, or any other image and likeness. In fact, he will not make decisions for the persons he is directing, but help them to fill out the picture, to have the background against which to make intelligent personal decisions. He will see his role as supportive rather than formative: to help the other person to face himself and then to become the self he was intended to be.

Tough Job

All this he will do by providing a continuing, completely confidential and empathetic atmosphere in which the young person may express himself as fully as possible, hence see himself and progressively know and accept himself according to his true capacities and limitations as a person of worth. He helps the young person to see the very real challenges that face him as one called to cooperate with Christ in his work of salvation, as a member of a special institute or as a future diocesan priest. (Some of this is taken, almost verbatim, from the Wernersville, Pa., meeting of the Committee of Spiritual Review, November 3-5, 1965.)

Thus, the spiritual director is a person who has gained some expertise in discernment—discernment of persons and discernment of spirits. He does not simply tell the person he is directing what "spirits" are moving him, but he does help him to understand what is going on, and then to go on and make up his own mind. This presupposes that the young person trusts him, both his capacity and his humaneness, and can be fully open with him. It also suggests that the role is not clinical but mutual; if the director must know diverse dimensions of the person he is helping, the latter must know him too. Dialogue means mutuality, here as elsewhere; indeed, here more than elsewhere. The director is more than a director; he must be a genuine, mature friend.

In this connection, Fr. John R. McCall, talking to religious on growth in mental health (Woodstock College, 1965), emphasized the necessity for "growth motivation" over "deficiency motivation." Deficiency motivation concentrates on things as they are, whereas growth motivation sees them as they might be. For a function of the spiritual director is "to help the man with his own vision." He should stimulate the individual's imagination, so that he will focus not so much on the world that he lives in as on the one that he wants to live in; not so much on the world of nature, as on the world that he is going to build. Since a vocation is built on faith—"the evidence of things unseen"—it cannot be sustained without a vision. Among other things, a vision can help one to stop worrying too much about what other people are thinking. "I stopped worrying about what other people were thinking of me," said Fr. McCall, "when I realized that they weren't thinking of *me* at all, but of what I was thinking about *them*."

Seminarians and religious live in a terribly competitive world. What is worse, this competitiveness is mostly unconscious. Everyone in the same group takes approximately the same course of studies. His performance is forever being compared to that of his peers. The superior may see him as a "soul"; his professor as a "brain"; his treasurer sees a "broad back" or a "mouth to feed." Each sees only a part of him as a person, not the whole person. Like inspectors on a conveyor-belt, each is concerned with his own specialty. The spiritual director is one person who must see him as a whole.

How To Love

The relationship, thus, becomes one of authentic love. For, as Viktor Frankl (*Man's Search for Meaning*, p. 176) expresses it, "Love is the only way to grasp another human being in the innermost core of his personality. No one can become fully aware of the very essence of another human being unless he loves him. By the spiritual act of love he is enabled to see the essential traits and features in the beloved person; and even more, he sees that which is potential in him, that which is not yet actualized but yet ought to be actualized. Furthermore, by his love, the loving person enables the beloved person to actualize these potentialities. By making him aware of what he can be and of what he should become, he makes these potentialities come true."

Or as Gabriel Marcel puts it (*Homo Viator*, p. 49), "To love anybody is to expect something from him, something which can neither be defined nor foreseen; it is at the same time in some way to make it possible for him to fulfill this expectation." Introspection will tell us that this is true, and that only the great expectations of those that we know truly love us ever help us to become what we should become. A level of self-denying love is, in fact, the only safeguard against turning direction into domination or crude manipulation.

What Can Be Done?

Little wonder that qualified spiritual directors are in such demand. Among the recommendations of the Santa Clara Conference are the following: That in houses where a large number of seminarians or young religious live there should be at least one specially skilled and trained spiritual director, in addition to a generous list of part-time spiritual directors; the men should be free to choose the one with whom they can deal most effectively, and the superior should know who each one's spiritual director is. That one university should develop a program of special training for spiritual directors, and that it should offer a number of summer institutes for priests already at work who wish to improve their competence. That spiritual directors (of a given area or congregation) should meet together at least annually. That new approaches should be encouraged, such as group dynamics, encounters, T-groups, sensitivity training. That spiritual directors should not only attend to individuals, but should make it their concern to help interpret the work of the Spirit in the community as such and make suitable recommendations to the superior (making sure, of course, that confidential information is kept confidential). That institutes should work to develop a spirituality appropriate to the American scene, and concern themselves with adapting the spirituality of other times and places to our own.

Whatever our apostolate, the main business we are in is spirituality—understood in a Christian not a dualistic sense. Nothing else we can do will ever matter as much as what we do toward helping priests and religious of the future to develop into mature, self-giving Christians.

The spiritual director, like any good teacher, must aim to make himself unnecessary.

VII
Obedience
and Authority

PERHAPS no area of religious life or the priesthood affords more problems than that of the apparent conflict between mature freedom and authority. We hear more and more about man's coming of age—hence his freedom. We know, too, that obedience is a vow approved by the Church for people committed to Christ's service, and that authority is its correlative. How to reconcile freedom and authority? In all candor it must be granted that we are not in possession of a full theology of freedom and authority. Accordingly, this chapter will only discuss, as frankly as possible, some of the problems and some lines of solution in the practical order. They are also treated in the chapters on Commitment, Spiritual Direction, Community and Personal Development.

First we look at obstacles from the viewpoint of the one obeying. When he looks at his "superior" (unfortunate word, but still in use) he senses certain discrepancies between the visible person and the invisible God whom the superior, in some way, represents. The almighty, omnicompetent, omniscient and infallible God of philosophy and theology is deeply veiled behind a weak, not always competent, not always right human being. Even if he tries to twist his thinking into denying the obvious —as he should not do, but often thinks he is supposed to do—he still cannot come up with the God-image he hoped to find. This is the case even when his superior is in every way superior, a rare paragon of goodness, wisdom, prudence, creativity, courage and the like. He still disappoints.

The superior's problem, aside from normal human limits, lies in the fact that he was never trained for his job. The Santa Clara Conference expressed this pointedly: "There is a serious need to select superiors psychologically capable of listening well and with obvious respect for every member of their community." For, in fact, if such a superior does emerge, it is because he was discovered, not prepared. I have been told by more than one provincial that he had never received the slightest hint of his impending appointment until three or four days before the axe fell. Thereupon, the poor appointee had barely time to pack his belongings, much less to study the constitutions of his order, do any consultation or even any reflection, before plunging into the herculean task. In no other important enterprise, surely not in big business or the academic world, does this type of thing often happen. A future executive goes through a sort of apprenticeship, through various stages of junior executive tasks, before being given anything like full charge.

An added tension lies in the ambiguity of his role. He is expected to be a religious superior, with all that implies; he is forced to be an administrator, financier, fundraiser, public relations man, and more. When can he find time to listen with anything like the attention or span of interest that his community needs? Little wonder that caught up in this maelstrom of conflicting duties, he becomes cross, edgy, inclined to take short cuts and minimize the importance of the individuals under him. A breakdown, or at least a jamming, in communications is likely to follow. In a word, we expect too much of superiors, and many superiors expect too much of themselves.

In fact, superiors who have been compelled by the system to assume this multi-faceted role find themselves employing bureaucratic techniques in a desperate effort to govern well. They multiply structures, adding to centralization, perpetuating the system and further complicating it. In such a maze, the superior often finds it hard to assume his true role: that of dynamic, charismatic leader. The structure becomes so opaque that he can hardly see through it, much less break through it. His vision, on every level, becomes dimmed by immediate responsibilities that never allow a feeling of space or focus.

So it is that he may be tempted to carry the burden alone, reluctant about delegating or sharing responsibility. Hampered by the existing situation, he may withdraw more and more from the community and give the impression of being haughty, unwilling and even incapable of dialoguing with the persons who make up the community. He may project an appearance of dishonesty in his day-to-day dealings, since he cannot communicate directly.

In any case, since he hasn't enough time to know the members of his community, they are bound to wonder how he can govern them with a wise and prudent exercise of authority. All too frequently, superiors seem to vacillate between a weak position of abdication, apparently fearing the loss of the community's esteem or affection, and a position of ruthless domination, as they can see no other interpretation of the will of God but their own. This apart from the credibility gap caused by fear that superiors may use, in a haphazard way, information that was given in confidence.

Problems of Superiors

Now we may look at obstacles from the superior's viewpoint. Many find evidence of an attitude, strongest among some young religious, that one may do everything not explicitly forbidden by the superior, as though the rules were *merely* guidelines, checkpoints, directives, but in no sense a control for their actions. This mentality tends to regard rules as stultifying and impractical at best.

Superiors are often worried about a tendency to employ the method of group pressure. In an age when protest marches and demonstrations are increasingly a fact of American life, some superiors look upon any community representation as a form of coercion, an attempt to force surrender to a mindless mob. They also see an internal conflict between personal development and the obligation of obedience. They fear that men all too often do not realize that freedom is responsibility rather than directionless spontaneity. Indeed, some superiors wonder if there is not some defect in the training of obedient religious, since there appears such a discrepancy between profession and practice.

So much for the problems, which could be expanded at considerable length. Now for some possible lines of solution.

Training for Superiors

Potential superiors should be given the opportunity of formal training before they are assigned to positions of authority. Such preparation should include both courses and programs devised for future leaders as well as various types of internships which can be provided both within and outside institutions of the particular religious congregation or order. This will require considerable cooperation between and among the orders, since no single order possesses a monopoly of talent or experience.

Since the burdens of superiors, especially higher superiors, are very heavy, specific steps should be taken to relieve official leaders of those time-consuming duties which hinder their effectiveness. In general, this can be achieved by the delegation of responsibilities. Such delegation will provide the superior with more freedom to assume his role of coordinator and source of inspiration and enthusiasm. His staff, especially at the higher level, should include several persons highly trained in various areas of concern and responsibility.

Further, superiors should take time out to assess their personal use of time: to find out, for example, how many hours in a normal working day are spent on trivia or details that could be effectively delegated.

The time saved by delegation can then be turned to the more important area of personal contact. The function of the dynamic leader is a proper balance between administrator and listener. He must be readily available, willing and able to be approached. At the same time, he must find time for thought, reflection, projection, vision. For his job is both short-range and long-range. He must not only be honest with his men, but must make it transparent that he is honest, that he takes them seriously, that he recognizes the stake that they have in the total enterprise.

The sad fact is that so frequently in this age of change, superiors follow rather than lead. Sometimes, indeed, they have trouble even following. In some places dialogue has broken down, when members of the community have despaired, perhaps over hastily, at their superiors' unwillingness or inability to respond to the signs of the times. Especially today the superior must have sufficient leisure ("sabbath" as we call it in the next chapter on Prayer) to study the documents of renewal and understand their underlying theology. In this he must not be outdistanced by his community.

Authority as Love

The contemporary theology of authority, incomplete as it may be, situates the problem within the New Testament themes of love and service. In the past, the nature of religious authority has been obscured by the actual practice of this authority, and the question of what authority *can do* has been quickly answered by what authority *has done*. Authority has tended to be based on power. This is true enough, provided the power is love, the only New Testament basis. Even the power to command and coerce, whenever it has to be used, must both be and be seen to be an exercise of loving service for the good of the individual and the community.

Love has its own way of commanding and coercing. This art, so necessary for the exercise of authority, must be practiced by every superior with a faith grounded in a genuine understanding of the Gospel. Texts so frequently neglected, but of the greatest importance for this understanding, are, for example: "The first among you must be as a slave" (Luke 22,26); "The Son of Man has come not to be served but to serve" (Mark 10,45); the washing of the disciples' feet (John 13,1-20), and Christ's explicit interpretation, "You ought also to wash each other's feet."

Time spent in reflection on these and other texts concerning the use of authority as loving service will help to Christianize what might otherwise be a naked use of power. It will help superiors to see in their fellow members persons to be loved and served, not pawns to be moved at will, or objects to be manipulated and controlled. Hence they will eagerly abandon any vestigial symbols of feudal power, such as places of honor for themselves or obsequious postures of reverence on the part of their fellow members.

Call for Dialogue

While all serious religious (and, indeed, all priests) are perfectly aware that the superior is in a unique position of ultimate signal caller, as mature human beings they rightly maintain that the superior should employ the wealth of experience, information and judgment constantly at his disposal. A good superior, in fact, will foster an atmosphere of refreshing and illuminating dialogue within the group. Such dialogue within all religious communities, large and small, is (as the Santa Clara Conference insisted) indispensable. This goal imposes a serious obligation on superiors to create the necessary climate and occasions of dialogue, and on members to participate courageously, freely, openly. For the person who stands apart from the community in its efforts at

dialogic renewal has no right to pass judgment on
these efforts.

But persons, too, must be dialogic, that is open to
dialogue. Most of all, the superior must be dialogic, as
the leader of dialogue. As Reuel Howe has pointed out
so well in his volume, *The Miracle of Dialogue*, such a
person must be total and authentic, open, disciplined and
related. He must be totally present to the men he is
listening to, and not running off on mental errands, not
so anxiety-bound that he can't grasp what he is hearing.
"He is able to learn as well as to teach, to be loved as
well as to love, to be served as well as to serve." He is just
as willing to reveal himself to others as to hear their
revelation. He must not be fearful about how his contribution is going to be received. Obedience only thrives in
an atmosphere of trust. The disciplined person makes his
contribution only in response to the contribution of
others, and he does not pursue a preconceived monologue
as though they had not spoken. His sense of relatedness
to the group will be seen in his awareness that all are
bound together and are dependent on one another.

Participation

This does not mean that congregations or orders that
are not governed by chapter should change into the capit-
ular form of governance; but it does mean that present
opportunities should be better used and other means
should be sought whereby religious can participate in
meaningful decisions, and indeed can participate in the
selection of their official leaders at every level. While
such a development is delicate, it seems none the less
imperative.

Since problems regarding obedience and authority

are not limited to any single religious order, it may be useful here to make available certain key statements on the subject made by the recent Thirty-First General Congregation of the Society of Jesus. These are taken from chapter 17, "The Life of Obedience." They represent a development in the theory of obedience and authority.

"After the example of Christ, whose place he holds, the superior should exercise his authority in a spirit of service, desiring not to be ministered to, but to serve. . . . He should exercise simplicity in his way of speaking, so that the friendly concord of Christ with his apostles may come to view. . . . Superiors should be appointed who, as far as possible, are gifted with true personal authority, so that they can inspire members to voluntary obedience, and so that they may willingly agree to be guided by them."

"In order that the superior may more easily discover the will of God, the superior should have at hand able advisers and should often consult them. He should also use the services of experts in reaching decisions on complex matters. . . . Besides, since all who work together in God's service are under the influence of the Holy Spirit and his grace, it will be advantageous to use their ideas and advice so as to understand God's will better. Superiors should readily and often ask for and listen to the counsel of their brothers."

Subsidiarity

"It is also advantageous that the superior leave much in his orders to the prudence of his confreres, making liberal use of the principle of subsidiarity."

(Here one is reminded of the practice of St. Ignatius Loyola, who made so much of the importance of obedience. One day Ignatius had ordered a local official to call all the fathers and brothers to engage in a work project. One of the young men proved to be psychologically un-equal to the task. Ignatius called the official and asked: "Don't you see that this novice is being tempted to go home when you put him at this work?" The official replied: "But you told me to have everybody in the house without exception work on the job." "But," rejoined Ignatius, "though I did say that, isn't it you who are in charge, and shouldn't you use some discretion?" The anecdote is included in *Finding God in All Things*, pp. 215-6, and is often used to illustrate the fact that obedience does not imply the abdication of discretion or good sense.)

"This truly spiritual government, whereby we are directed by superiors with discerning love rather than through external laws, supposes communication between the two which is as plain and open as possible. . . . The religious should try to make himself known, with his gifts and limitations, his desires, difficulties and ideas, through a continuing, confiding, familiar and candid dialogue, about which the superior is held to strict se-crecy. . . . This will constitute the dialogue that is funda-mental and essential for the healthy progress of our society."

"Obedience does not take away, but rather by its very nature and perfection supposes in the subject the obliga-tion of personal responsibility and the spirit of ever seek-ing what is better." (nn. 6, 7, and 8)

Functions of Freedom

Regarding the tension between obedience and self-fulfillment, we may here present some insights of Fr.

John Courtney Murray, who studied the problem profoundly in the last years of his life. In his article, "Freedom, Authority, Community" (quoted in the chapter on Community), he explains: "It is sometimes stated that obedience is a bar to the self-fulfillment of the individual. The statement may conceal a fallacy—an individualistic concept of self-fulfillment, and a failure to realize that self-fulfillment is not simply an affair of freedom but also an affair of community. Briefly, self-fulfillment is the achievement of freedom for communion with others. Therefore, it is also somehow an affair of obedience to authority; for in every kind of community there is always some kind of authority."

There are, in Fr. Murray's view, three functions of Christian freedom. "The primary function may be called, for the sake of a name, charismatic. It is the free response of the community and of all its members to the unitive function of authority, whose initial act is the invitation to dialogue (on which the Council more than once laid emphasis).... The second may be called executive. It corresponds to the decisive and directive functions of authority. It also corresponds to the formal moral notion of freedom as duty—the freedom whereby one does what one ought to do.... Obedience, as an act of Christian freedom, even when it is sacrificial (as part of the paschal mystery)—especially when it is sacrificial—is always the way to self-fulfillment. It is the expression of one's self-awareness that one is called to be in the image of the Son Incarnate, who freely gave his life for the many and thus went his way to the self-fulfillment that was his resurrection.... The third function of Christian freedom may have to go without a name, unless one calls it self-corrective.... It is the Christian rejection of the temptation, inherent in the psychological notion of freedom as choice, to 'use your freedom as an opportunity for the flesh' (Gal. 5,13). It is the act whereby Christian freedom stands forth in all its evangelical newness, unique among all the modalities of freedom that men have claimed or hoped for or dreamed of."

Obedience, like the rest of religious life, makes no sense—other than crudely pragmatic—unless it is situated in the Christian, that is, the paschal, context. For even when as much as possible of the mystification shrouding it has been dissipated, there remains mystery. This does not free us from the further task of theological understanding and elucidation, nor may we eschew the effort at making obedience as reasonable and functional as possible. But the final word will have to be more than rational; it will be in terms of faith, hope and love.

VIII
Prayer

"THERE LIES our whole vocation: to listen to him who generates the Word, and to live thereby." The quotation is from an anonymous spiritual writer.

If anything can be said to be obvious about the life of religious or priests it is that prayer holds a high place in it. Indeed, the rest of the Church looks on them as preeminently persons of prayer. The request "Pray for me," either in this banal formulation or in some less direct or more sophisticated one, is heard again and again by priest, seminarian, religious. It's the matter he's expected to be professional at.

Hardly less obvious is the fact of a major reorientation with regard to prayer in the life of the Church. Less than ever is *prayer* identified with *prayers*. The movement is more toward spontaneous and flexible prayer, away from rigid forms or set times. Prayer is to be experienced as "personally meaningful" (to quote probably every religious conference held in recent years), and not simply performed out of a sense of duty or assignment. Perhaps most characteristic of all the new emphases is the view of prayer as essentially social, communal, re-

lated to the world of persons. And this applies even to
prayer in solitude, solitude seen as Christian, hence as
related to the Whole Christ.

In almost every document of Vatican II we sense that
the Church has opened out to the world. Nine days after
the Council opened, the fathers issued a most cordial
"Message to Humanity" in which they "humbly and ar-
dently call for all men to work along with us in building
up a more just and brotherly city in this world." Again
and again, thereafter, the Council showed an increasing
recognition of the Incarnation as a mystery of divine
identification with, and involvement in, the lives of men.
This means (in the Santa Clara Conference's terms) "that
the discovery of God and the growing awareness of the
presence of the three divine persons, which is the root of
any relationship to them in prayer, must occur in one's
experience of people."

Just about everything we have, we have from others.
Our first knowledge and experience of God comes from
parents and others who love us. Throughout life people
we encounter are, more or less formally, "sacraments"
of God's presence: that is, they are signs that not only
point to God and reveal him to us, but actually render
him present in a most personal way. Prayer is, thus, a
sort of illumined reflection on our own experience, especially our interpersonal experience, since that is our
basic and most human experience.

Prayer as Response

Today, more commonly than in the recent past,
Christians see prayer not so much as a striving, a boot-
strap-self-lifting, but rather as a response in faith to God

constantly revealing himself. This, in fact, may be the key to prayer: a dynamic notion of revelation, God coming to us, ourselves responding to him. For God's revelation is in fact a dynamic, never-finished process. It comes to us through Scripture, the sacraments and the teaching of the Church; but it also comes to us continuously in life situations, not just bits and snatches, but the whole world process as we experience it.

Scripture and the sacraments are, to be sure, especially transparent instances of God's initiative: Scripture gives the experience of God's people as it once happened, while the sacraments are the experience of God's people here and now. But the Spirit is constantly revealing himself through the people of God, who have received him.

Another profound truth of the faith that has come into sharp focus in recent years is the central role of the Resurrection. More and more we are aware of the risen Christ, living now, and present now in his people. Prayer, accordingly, tends to be more paschal-oriented than formerly; indeed, more closely related to prayer as was common in the early Church, with its stress on the Resurrection. Many people today find it more effective to direct their prayer to Christ as he is now than to re-create imaginatively the Jesus of two thousand years ago.

At the same time, while there may be said to be a special presence of the Holy Spirit to be discerned in "the signs of the times," this does not preclude his direct, personal contact with the individual. Accordingly, it would be appropriate to allow considerable flexibility and accommodation to individuality, and in fact to encourage them. For there are, as salvation history shows, many valid forms of prayer. Our first obligation in prayer (as Urs von Balthasar states in *Prayer*, p. 12) is to "listen to God's word and then, subsequently, through that word, learn how to answer."

This listening stance is surely the first preparation to contemplation, whether the contemplation be related to action or not. Whether the religious is to be "contemplative in action" (to use the Ignatian phrase) or otherwise, contemplation involves a receptive and continued attention to all things in reality: to the word of God, to other persons, to the depths of reality.

Granted, there will be "family resemblances" within a given religious institute; it seems outside the spirit of Vatican II to force this family resemblance to obliterate individual styles of holiness or prayer. Again, the striking variety of types shown by the various saints of a given religious order reminds us that the Spirit breathes as he wills, even within a given institutional structure. Pluralism appears as much a mode of holiness as of human institutions.

Personally Meaningful

To return now to the phrase "personally meaningful." If prayer is not at least minimally personal it is not prayer at all, and if it is not meaningful it is to that extent null. Even before the reforms in the liturgy, people were always urged not merely to "hear" or "attend" Mass, but somehow to pray during it; and all manner of props and aids were offered in prayer manuals. Since the beginning of this century, there has been a constant, though at first slow, movement toward greater and fuller intelligibility and participation. Even so, for years Benediction was more popular among religious than Mass, precisely because it offered a clear, simple framework for personal, meaningful prayer. The same may be said of other devotions, with their strongly personal, indeed individualistic, flavor. Today's reaction in favor of the liturgy is not only the consequence of greater theological sophistication, but parallels closely the increasingly flexible structure of the liturgy.

Noncommital Prayers

Spontaneous prayer, whether within the liturgy or not, possesses a number of advantages. It can and often does flow from the person's inspiration of the moment, rather than follow predetermined formulae. But more importantly, spontaneous prayer helps us realize what we're doing. Familiar texts, be they even as hallowed as the Lord's Prayer itself, have a way of quickly losing their bite. Their problem is that they are too easy. They become, in the literal sense, noncommittal. Often, in fact, they are so high-flown as not really to touch us within. When we have to say what we mean, unsupported by memorized formulae, we come closer to commitment. We are more involved.

Thus it is that recent liturgical reforms have eliminated repetitions, on the principle that redundancy is ineffectual. One may, for example, say the Our Father once and mean it seriously. But the second or third time, it becomes, no longer the Our Father, but a verbal background to mental prayer or distractions. Long ago, thus, the endless sequence of Hail Mary's contained in the Rosary became precisely such a background against which one was expected to meditate on something else than what was being said. It was probably the principle of avoiding repetitiousness that caused the Church to allow communion only once a day. How could one rise to the level of intensity appropriate for such a sacrament

several times in one short span of time? Ask any priest
how much "devotion" he senses when he has to celebrate
several Masses in a row.

Praying Together

In recent years young religious have found an ancient
form of prayer particularly meaningful and personal. It
is the *collatio*: a group prayer during which each person
reads a few verses of Scripture and everyone reflects and
shares his reflections aloud. Often, too, the term *collatio*
is used more loosely as a synonym for informal group
prayer, much like the "group homily" or "shared reflections" at Mass (discussed in the following chapter). This
is not precisely the same as a "sensitivity session" or
"T-group," though it has something in common; nor is
it precisely the same as discussion, which is more apt for
problem solving. Again, the several procedures may over-
lap or at times coincide.

For those of us of a certain age, the idea of meditat-
ing in groups of two or more may seem self-contradic-
tory. We have been accustomed to treating such intimate
matters as prayer as altogether private; many of us even
find it embarrassing to share them with our confessor or
spiritual director. Not so, or at least not so frequently, is
this problem felt by younger religious or seminarians.
With a candor and outspokenness that sometimes appalls
us when we first encounter it, they find it helpful to pray
aloud in each other's company. Indeed, many find it the
most effective of all forms of prayer.

Another traditional style of prayer is the monastic
lectio divina, a quiet, recollected reading of Holy Scripture (or some commentary on Holy Scripture). The passage may be read over and over again—not in the

mechanical way described above—but in an earnest effort
to listen to the Spirit speaking through the word of God.
Today, with our developed understanding of the origin
of the New Testament, we can perhaps better sense the
appropriateness of various scriptural pericopes to our
own situation. As the early Church searched into its
experience of Christ and recalled the key episodes of his
life as they had bearing on its existential needs, so we
try to see their meaning in terms of our own needs.

A Place for Solitude

The stress on communal, social prayer does not at all
mean the abandonment of solitude. For, as spiritual
writers of all ages insist, there must always be an element of the desert in the Christian experience. Only,
Christian solitude (unlike that of certain Oriental reli-
gions) is not solitude *from* people but solitude *for* people.
Understood this way, it is not flight but a special type of
involvement. Granted that our first awareness of our own
personhood comes from interpersonal experience, this is
not to say all that needs to be said. For solitude is necessary for realization, to make realization truly personal.
It is even a condition for full development, a condition
for being a person at all. We are so bombarded by experiences, that without time for reflection—that is to say,
solitude—we have no way of understanding these experiences in depth. Instead of depth there remains only
shallowness.

A number of the vital religious thinkers of our day
have stressed this need: Max Picard, in *The World of
Silence*; Joseph Pieper, in *Leisure, the Basis of Culture*;
Romano Guardini, in a number of works, notably, *Medi-
tations before Mass*; Gabriel Marcel, in *The Mystery of*

Being. Marcel, in chapter 6, "Feeling as a Mode of Participation," points up the distinction between "contemplative" and "spectator," the latter being detached, neutral, not committed, while the contemplative is involved. "For somebody who floats on the surface of reality, or who, as it were, skims over the thin ice of that surface on skates," contemplation is inconceivable. In chapter 7, "Being in a Situation," he describes contemplation: "To contemplate is to ingather oneself in the presence of whatever is being contemplated." Yet this very "ingatheredness is not a state of abstraction from anything." Rather, it is "essentially a state in which one is drawing nearer something, without abandoning anything." In our age of activism, often characterized by feverishness, we are in special need of contemplation; otherwise, we cannot be "contemplatives in action" but simply active.

In fact, to be truly communal or social, whether in prayer or work, we need to be contemplative. For in an interpersonal encounter, each person brings his own personality to bear, sharing, charging, engaging. If the personality is superficial or diminished or blurred, no real contribution can be made, and one becomes parasitic rather than social. The example of Christ, withdrawing only for the sake of a greater unity, is applicable to today's apostle.

Dialogue with Books

Christian solitude allows for another kind of dialogue —dialogue with books. Principally, of course, this should be with the book of God's word. But others too, depending on one's education and taste, can be instrumental in helping one to achieve realization. The anonymous writer quoted at the beginning of this chapter has this to say: "One seeks in books that silence whence the words were born, which is those depths of the soul that no language can express, for they are beyond expression. It is here we touch what is measureless, eternal and divine in us."

Spiritual reading is today perhaps more urgently needed than ever, if only as countervalent to the ambient of mass media. Happily, more books treating of spiritual themes, and adapted to apostolically oriented men and women, are available today than at any time in the past. But even books without specifically religious themes can bestir one to contemplation: poems and other literature. It is not practicable to prescribe here since personal requirements vary so widely.

As we have described it, solitude implies a measure of silence. In Gironella's novel, *The Cypresses Believe in God*, Mosén Francisco is sagely counseling young Ignacio: "I would advise you to do one thing that may seem to you irrelevant: a silence cure. Try it, and tell me how it works out. Manage to go a few days, a couple of weeks, talking as little as possible. Work silently at the bank, study in silence, and economize on words as much as possible. You will see the effects. Almost immediately you will feel a greater serenity. You will find that you pay attention and see things much more clearly." Thus, silence—Christian silence—far from being egocentric, leads toward responsiveness—responsiveness to God's continuing presence in persons and the whole world process.

Keeping the Sabbath

A number of the most effective people I know make a great deal of what we may call a use of the Sabbath.

Overworked as most of us tend to be, we are menaced by a loss of vision. True, Sunday itself is very often the most hectic of days; if so, some other Sabbath must be taken. For we need a rhythm of activity and repose, of the intensely interpersonal and Christian solitude, if we are not to wither or atrophy.

We need to take thought, and this means "cultivating a habit of sustained reflection, of stepping back from immediate goods and enjoyments to see where they lead," as Robert O. Johann puts it. "It means refusing to endorse our initial reactions until their credentials have been checked and validated. . . . The aim of thought, then, is not to suppress spontaneity but, through enlarging its scope, to guard it from short-circuiting itself."

Thus, while spontaneity is a true value, paradoxically it is an elusive one. Everyone grants that five minutes of intense awareness of God, of absorbed listening to his revelation and summons, is worth ever so much more than hours of routine prayers. Yet, unless we do something to structure our lives, allowing regular periods for communal or solitary (in the sense described above) prayer, we shall seldom have leisure for earnest listening. True, an excess of automatism may, as Paul Tournier words it (in *The Meaning of Persons*), prove the tomb of the spiritual life. For like all life "it is made up of intermittent creative flashes and permanent automatisms." Some automatisms are needed to support and prolong these creative flashes, to be sure; and for certain types of persons they are particularly important, precisely to enlarge and safeguard spontaneity.

Yet, whether prayer is to be predominantly in company with others, or away from them, it remains communal, directed toward the world of persons. It is more a response than an initiative—which does not suggest that we do not need all the initiative possible to discover how we are to listen. There are, even within a given school of spirituality, many valid forms of prayer, many techniques and approaches. If anywhere, as children of God we are most entitled to freedom in the matter of our personal, growing, flexible response to his ever-present word.

A Time to Pray

And if there are many valid forms of prayer even within the same religious family, how much more freedom should there be with regard to the time of prayer. Some structure, granted, there must be as a corrective to inertia and as a supportive underpinning. And some explicitly community prayer is obviously a needed ingredient of religious life.

But it should be too obvious to need stating that not all prayer—least of all, all reflective prayer—needs to be done at one single time, in one single place. Prayer is the breath of spiritual life and must not be smothered by such rigidity. It is a commonplace of psychology that people have different rhythms of alertness: some are most fit in the morning, others at other times. To force every member of a community to pray inefficiently by being coerced to follow an inflexible schedule, regardless of personal need, is to turn prayer into sheer pelagian automatism. Prayer, to be sure, frequently requires effort. But if we make it a sort of enforced psychic callisthenics, a kind of will-training drill, we drain it of its deepest value. A certain feeling of space, roominess and fresh air is needed if prayer is to be an activity of the children of God.

IX
Liturgy

I T HAS not been many years, surely not more than a few
decades, since the term liturgy connoted churchly
propriety, the panoply surrounding the Blessed Sacrament, a cultic style of life, or the like. Future priests
looked forward to the moment when they would (in the
rhetoric of the day) call the Second Person of the Blessed
Trinity down to the altar, an altar bedizened with as
many baroque trappings as possible. Other religious cen-
tered their lives on certain privileged moments like Benediction or the Elevation at Mass.

Thus, it would not be true to suggest that the liturgy
meant nothing to them. It means a great deal, in fact;
and if these preceding sentences seem a gross caricature,
it is because we have come such a long way in the past
few years. Several papal encyclicals, but most of all the
Council's *Constitution on the Sacred Liturgy* changed
and enormously enriched everyone's grasp of what liturgy
is all about.

The great majority of today's religious belong to
institutes that arose during the Middle Ages or the Coun-

ter Reformation. During both these periods, as Fr. Josef Jungmann has pointed out, "men focused their attention, not so much on the glorified Christ as he is portrayed in St. Paul and many Fathers, but rather on the historical Christ as he went through the events or 'mysteries' of his life on earth." This corresponds to periods when the liturgy, largely performed in a remote language and with gestures and ceremonies whose meaning had been lost or transformed, tended to be something to be watched rather than shared in. Devotions filled the void, as witness the stress on Rosary, devotion to the Five Wounds, the Stations of the Cross, the Crib, and finally toward the end of the 17th century, the Sacred Heart as the center or focus of all these concepts.

In contrast, the spirituality found in the documents of Vatican II is that of the liturgico-pastoral movement of our era. It is based on a return to the primitive sources, to Scripture and the history of salvation (how many of us had heard the phrase "salvation history" before, say, 1960?). In this history, Christ's earthly life is indeed a part, but only a part which is continued in his glorified life and in his mystical body through which he is now operating. In other words, this spirituality centers its attention on the paschal mystery and on the presence of Christ. This presence is, of course, not merely in the Blessed Sacrament, but also in the other sacraments, in his word by which he speaks when the Scriptures are read, especially in the liturgy; but he is also present when "two or three are gathered in my name." (See *Constitution on the Sacred Liturgy*, especially n. 7.)

Liturgy and the Young

This fuller understanding of liturgy, which seems also

closer to that of the early Church, has very much captured the imagination of younger religious and seminarians today. It is not merely or principally because they are less formal or ritualistic than most of their elders. They have had wider exposure to Holy Scripture, to salvation history, to sacramental theology. Further, they are intensely conscious of social values and dialogue. So it is that liturgy, understood in Vatican II terms, is no longer something mainly awesome, so vertical and elevated as to seem more a climax or reward of spiritual life; rather, it is the very center, the focus of that spiritual life. To them it is, granted, "the summit toward which the activity of the Church is directed," as the Council words it; but it is much more, as the Council also puts it, "the source from which all its power flows."

No sociological study of liturgical and devotional attitudes among young religious and seminarians has yet been taken. However, preliminary to the Santa Clara Conference, a serious effort was made to produce a profile of American Jesuits, based on responses to an elaborate 212-table questionnaire (printed under the title *Survey of American Jesuits*, by Eugene Gerard and John Arnold). Since 85 per cent of the scholastics (who are both seminarians and religious with vows, and may thus be taken as somewhat representative of both groups) responded, (some 2000 men in all), we may be interested in noting their attitudes toward liturgy and devotions. While over 87 per cent of scholastics found the Mass quite "meaningful," only 8 per cent found the Rosary so (and 58 per cent "not at all"); further, the ratios for devotion to the Sacred Heart and toward the Blessed Virgin (11 and 13 per cent respectively for quite meaningful) showed the same overwhelming difference between response to the liturgy and response to traditional devotions.

A Meaningful Liturgy

If we may extrapolate from this sampling of 2,000 seminarian-religious, it should be plain that the Mass (which is just about the only liturgical experience that enters their lives daily) is crucially significant, and so far as we may project, will be crucially significant to seminarians and religious for the foreseeable future. At this, some superiors may be inclined to sigh: "At last, something hopeful!" As I see it, however, the *Survey* just quoted poses as many problems as it offers grounds for hope. For it seems to me beyond cavil that the enthusiasm shown for the Mass would have been unthinkable save for the vigorously adapted liturgical style now common in all the Jesuit seminaries I have visited. Were the liturgy not seen as meaningful, if it did not "turn" the young men "on," they would not have responded as they did. For, as Fr. Joseph Wall put it unambiguously: "If our liturgy is not meaningful to those with whom and for whom we work, it is bad liturgy."

This is by no means to propose an anarchic free-for-all in the matter of liturgical adaptation. We have all been subjected to horror stories about secret, gnostic, underground Masses, celebrated capriciously according to the most whimsical vagaries of wild young priests, be they Dutch or American. Regrettably, the press has done its utmost to sensationalize such Masses, and there is the classic case of *Paris-Match* dedicating a cover story to a case in Holland. Upon checking the story in Holland, however, I discovered that the entire story had been "set up" by the irresponsible writer, pictures and all. In fact, the Masses I witnessed in Holland, both in churches and in private groups, struck me as entirely appropriate and adjusted to the pastoral needs of the groups being served.

Need for Adaptation

I am not proposing a catch-all formula for liturgical adaptation in the typical parish situation. However, it seems that experience shows no serious danger in the widest possible latitude within the seminary or religious community setting. For there, built-in controls and structures can insure taste, balance and judgment. Particularly where superiors take initiative themselves and engage in serious dialogue with community leaders, interesting, diversified, functional liturgies can be worked out. The Santa Clara Conference consensus paper on liturgy earnestly exhorts superiors "not to content themselves with a permissive attitude in the matter of liturgical adaptation and experiment, but to take the lead." And this because "liturgical adaptation and experiment are of such pressing apostolic importance."

Several difficulties have to be faced at this point. One is the matter of legislation. In those dioceses where the entire liturgical thrust of Vatican II (not merely its letter but its thrust toward real change) is looked upon with suspicion and acted upon with extreme reluctance, seminarians and religious have a hard time. On the one hand, they try, in the spirit of Vatican II, to see the Bishop as their great liturgist; on the other, they find it shocking when curial regulations are so restrictive as (so they understandably feel) to "quench the Spirit." Unless their superiors persist, like the woman in the Gospel, in importuning until a favorable response comes, some confidence may be lost. It would be good if the highest superiors, especially if they are Ordinaries themselves, would "enter into dialogue with the local Ordinary" (as the Santa Clara Conference recommends).

Above all, among priests and religious there should be a climate of trust. We are not rash when we trust those who, in all seriousness, try to make the liturgy more prayerful, more communitarian, more understandable, more relevant to present-day young religious. But we are, so it seems to me, very rash when we appear distrustful of them. Far better a few gauche excesses committed by the over-eager than self-defeating over-caution, which can easily lead to discouragement or disgust.

What Can Be Done Now?

Even so, if after all efforts to secure authorization for liturgical adaptation have failed, a vast amount can still be done within present structures. As long as an initiative (be it understood that such an initiative is sensible) is not explicitly forbidden, it should be taken as allowed. For example, many communities are small enough to allow shared reflections (or "dialogue homily") in place of an official homily; these, in fact, often prove to be far more effective and to the point.

This may be the moment to say something about *creative* implementation, over and above the mere simple implementation of current liturgical directives. The phrase is being currently used by respected canon lawyers as a corrective to accusations about departures from rubrics or experimentation. Why, for example, can't we use bread that looks like bread, thus fulfilling the need for a sign that signifies? Many recipes are available for bread that will qualify as both valid and licit for the eucharistic celebration. The only explicit norm given is that the bread be of such size and shape as befits so great a sacrament. The shared reflections we mentioned above are another instance of creative implementation. Further, more than one professor of canon law insists that the examples given in the documents regarding communion under both species are only examples, and should not be taken as the only cases where it may be allowed. All restrictive laws, in any case, are to be applied generously and in the direction of freedom. The fact that abuses *can* sometimes occur must never so intimidate us as to have us lean over backwards into the greater abuse of inflexibility, forgetting that the "sacraments are for men not men for the sacraments."

Another practical example of creative implementation is the arrangement of the liturgical setting, so as to make it conducive to the worship of this particular group. The simple use of the vernacular in a setting adjusted to older forms of worship betrays an incomplete understanding of liturgy—which involves the total sign, not tokenism. Even older chapels can be re-toned to fit modern needs by the use of banners and disposable liturgical art of all sorts, suiting different feasts and seasons, and providing an atmosphere of warmth rather than of the morgue. Even in parishes, which by their size lend themselves less to creative implementation, things can be done. For example, appropriate hymns may be used in place of entrance, offertory and communion antiphons.

Further, something needs to be said about the cautionary directives issued from Rome with regard to implementation and experimentation. (Obviously, they do not apply to either simple or creative implementation.) What these directives seem to mean is the exclusion of irresponsible, whimsical, capricious innovations done without expertise or the authority of liturgical history and precedent; priests are forbidden to introduce any definitive changes; priests are not to engage in public experimentation in the type of parochial situation where this could cause confusion or scandal. On the other hand, as is suggested in an editorial for the June 17, 1967 issue of *America*, the documents do not "forbid prudent, careful, controlled experimentation with liturgical forms." (A similar development of these ideas may be found in the talk by Fr. Thomas Ambrogi, professor of liturgy at Woodstock College, given at the 1967 Liturgical Week and printed in the Proceedings.)

In communities where a number of priests are available, small group liturgies often prove especially valuable. They offer a good chance for members of the community to get together on a very personal level and to express to themselves and to each other what they are and aspire to be at the deepest levels. Small group liturgies are a valid counterfoil to excessive size, where the individual becomes engulfed in the group. More importantly, they are effective in offering interpersonal spiritual experiences in depth. This cannot be provided otherwise, either in large groups or in private prayer.

We Need Rhythm

At the same time, it should be remembered that neither a seminary nor a religious house is a monolithic, undifferentiated unity, though, most unfortunately, some give that appearance. Consequently, as the Santa Clara paper expresses it, "a rhythm between liturgical celebrations at which the entire community is urged to be present and eucharistic liturgies in small groups should be fostered." For though a large house is really more

than one community (community here taken in a sociological sense) and each of these communities should have
a liturgical expression at least occasionally, such a house
is also, in some ways, one community and should have a
liturgical expression as a whole. The rhythm between
large and small liturgies cannot be pre-established, but
should be fitted to possibilities and real needs.

What is more, neither religious houses nor (still less)
seminaries should be thought of as fully self-contained,
nor should their liturgical expressions be so. At least
occasionally it would be good for all to participate in the
liturgy of the wider community, say, the parish or university complex. No one, not even in the most enclosed
convent, is a member of only one community, and there
should be ways of expressing this larger unity in worship.
For if our life, and every sociological reality about it, is
not related to God in liturgy, then that much of our life
is diminished and trivialized.

The matter of rhythm in liturgy extends even farther
than this. At least for fellow Jesuits (and how applicable
this will be for others I have no way of saying), the Conference had this to say: "The Conference believes that
daily attendance at Mass, or daily celebration for those
who are priests, is so close to the intimate personal piety
of each man that it is counter-productive to make it a
matter of strict obligation. The rule of the Society in this
regard should not be misinterpreted as an edict. The same
should be said, for the same reasons, of the rule of con-
·fession every eight days."

This will surely sound startling to many, accustomed
as many of us have been to a strict regimen of daily Mass.
It presupposes an attitude of maturity on the part of
some, and of trust on the part of others, that has often

been lacking in religious houses and seminaries. It further presupposes mutuality between superiors and their younger companions, a complete interchange of confidence, and a consequent responsibility carried not by any single person but by all. It would be as naive to suppose that somehow laziness had been exorcized from the present generation and that no correctives were needed, as to suppose that every detail of spiritual growth had to be watched and controlled. As regimentation decreases, trust and self-discipline must increase.

Higher superiors have a responsibility that arises from all we have said about liturgy: to make sure that other houses, to which the young religious or seminarians will go after their early years of development, are not regressive in liturgical attitudes. Otherwise these young persons will have the deeply disturbing experience of confronting a community attitude contrary to their own deepest Christian convictions. This presupposes some program of on-going renewal among older members.

Change: A Way of Life

However the problem of daily Mass is solved, the following points will, I submit, enter into the solution. Within the past few years, young Christians have experienced the liturgy in exciting new ways. As psychologist Fr. John R. McCall has reminded us, "Everything for them comes down to personal experience, and religion is the most personal experience of all." Further, for them, change "is a way of life" and "not a temporary process between two permanent plateaus of stability." The issue, I believe, is not that of novelty for novelty's sake, as is sometimes charged, but a needed sense of newness for which they find scriptural warrant in him who said "I have come to make all things new."

Thus (as I have tried to express in *Our Changing Liturgy*), though a rhythm of liturgical change is a psychological and spiritual need for us all, it is ever so much more so for those who have grown up in a mobile, nomadic, almost kaleidoscopic way of life. Tradition is not an automatic value, in their book; indeed, it is a non-value to them if it appears to be stifling or even simply routine. Brought up in a climate of questioning, searching, non-authoritarianism, today's young Christians want and need to pray in ways that are at least partly their own.

If the chapel's appointments, the music, the style of celebration does not "speak to them," they will seek elsewhere. Spontaneity tends to be equated with sincerity, ritualism with prissiness; merely token changes are likely to evoke not enthusiasm but mutterings like "big deal" or "Mickey Mouse." If the liturgy is to be taken seriously, its style must clearly be seen as seriously adapted to them and not simply to their ancestors. Petrified customs are all right for students of archaeology to examine; they should have nothing to do with real prayer.

We cannot, then, simply impose identical, inflexible ceremonies on today's youth and expect a true response. If we are to help them (and ourselves, no less) achieve a needed sense of ritual, we must not confuse ritual with routine, but in the words of Dr. Samuel Miller, must try to lift our liturgical actions to "a new level of clarity and transparency." For it is no solution at all to throw up our hands and assert that young people today refuse all ritual. They are quite as ready as the Little Prince to accept the sage fox's advice in the fable: "We need rites . . . rites are things that make one day different from another."

But the rites must symbolize and in some way articulate our personal feelings, not merely those of the ancients.

Movement Must Move

Only if we grow in an understanding of tradition as speaking to the present and make this relevance transparent to today's young religious and tomorrow's priests, will the Catholic tradition-sense be more than antiquarianism. The present-day agitation and concern-for-relevance can, in fact, produce among some of us what Fr. Robert Hovda calls "a kind of naive and superficial equation between the notion of an avant-garde (which the Church always needs desperately) and a reactionary nihilism disclaiming any roots, any relations with the past (which we do not need at all)." (*Worship*, 1967, p. 519) But this requires a great deal of patient dialogue. If the liturgical movement is to remain alive, it must move; the renewal must continue to be new.

Now, especially, that we have almost the entire liturgy in the vernacular, the need for freshness must not be thought to be allayed once for all. Rather the contrary. For as long as the Mass was hidden in the incense of a hieratic, half-grasped tongue, the pious imagination could meander at will in quest of devotion. With everything intelligible, however, monotony will quickly set in and it will soon be as hard to be attentive at Mass as during the Rosary. As Archbishop Paul J. Hallinan cautioned his priests (November 2, 1967): "Our people should not be encouraged to think that the liturgy changes are 'over'. . . . We must help them, not by soothing them that it will all be over soon, nor by falsely agreeing with them that we, faithful stewards of Christ and his Church, feel the same way."

If many older Catholics are disturbed by liturgical change, many younger ones are even more troubled by whatever smacks of reluctance or distrust. Vatican II caused a flood of rising expectations especially among the vibrant, thoughtful, eager younger generation. The future belongs to them, and to the next generation and the next; if we expect them to be sympathetic to us, to our older style of worship, we must lead the way in openness, empathy and unfeigned trust. After all, they have shown trust and taken brave risks in venturing into our way of life.

X
Poverty

THE OLD canard "you religious vow poverty, we practice it" has long been more than a point-scorer in
banter between religious and others. Not only is it an
epigram hard to rebut in the same number of words; it
touches on a sensitive nerve. For most of us with vows
of poverty feel at least occasional twitches of malaise as
we note the "hundredfold" that seems to go with vowed
poverty. It seems too abundant a hundredfold, indeed,
especially when we visit the "inner city" or work there.

The literature on religious poverty does little to dis-
sipate our qualms. We are still (as the Santa Clara Conference granted) "in search of a fully satisfactory view."
Indeed, "whatever theory we follow or whatever our
practice may be, we have in our lives an important area
of lived contradiction." Accordingly, the present treatment will be less than satisfactory. Yet, not to have all the
answers or not to have a total synthesis is not the same
as having no answers at all, or no hints of possible direc-
tions, or no lines of further examination and discussion.

A problem with poverty, as it is often lived, is that of
breeding irresponsibility. The religious can act as if he

were emancipated from insecurity, from the need of creating the conditions of his life. He risks becoming less a person, a sort of parasite on society. As Fr. John Courtney Murray put it in a classic talk on the vows, the religious declines the encounter "with the earth." It is a real risk: becoming mature without engaging in the struggles that normally help bring about maturity.

Poverty in Affluent America

In our affluent American society the risk is exacerbated and complicated. For the first time in the history of the Church, we are called on to practice poverty in an economy of overwhelming, if unequally distributed, abundance. Hitherto human society has normally existed in an economy of scarcity; today the standard of living, notably in America, is incredibly high. Most of us come from families who enjoy this unparalleled (in terms of the past and of the majority of men living) wealth. We remain part of society, yet we are called to follow closely him who was identified with the poor and who summoned us to "leave all things."

We are also caught "in the bind" of another rather typically American conflict: between the ideals of American efficiency and of religious poverty. We know that efficiency is a value; it fits in with the sound principle of taking apt means to achieve the right end. The American religious has some notion of time being money, aware that it is possible to be penny wise and pound foolish. Isn't it "against poverty" not to use the latest in efficiency tools and techniques, not to be comfortable enough to do one's best work, to spend time doing lowly tasks when one could be doing work that would accomplish the farther and wider good? It would be disingenuous to pretend that no conflict existed. Can one be really apostolic and really poor?

Further, today's young religious, as we have often noted, is contemptuous of tokenism. It smacks of phoniness to talk of poverty and yet have all one needs. When the young religious first encounters what are called in some communities "first-class feasts" he is at least mildly shocked: can this be what poverty means? He hears a great deal about "poverty of dependence"—which means that he can have just about anything, so long as he gets permission for it. Why not call things by their right name? Does it mean "community of supply" to meet our every demand?

Then, too, he faces an added complication in the fact that community poverty is by definition communal and becomes associated with the demands of Christian charity itself. Supposing—as I believe we have warrant to do— that many, especially many younger religious, would prefer to have simpler meals, less posh living quarters and the like: as soon as others voice contrary opinions, what can they do? Perhaps these others do need more than they personally do, and it would be uncharitable to force a sterner way on them. In any case, they feel that to speak up in favor of austerity would be to appear to question their confreres' sincerity.

Yet, the teaching Church continues to laud and reinforce religious poverty: it "provides a witness which is highly esteemed, especially today"; "communities as such should aim at giving a kind of corporate witness to their own poverty"; "religious poverty requires more than limiting the use of possessions to the consent of superiors"; "religious ought to be poor both in fact and in spirit" (Vatican II's *Decree on the Appropriate Renewal of the Religious Life*, n. 13). So it is that, regardless of our speculative impasse, we must find day-to-day, *de facto* solutions.

Personal and Communitarian

These solutions will have to be both personal and communitarian. The individual can find constant chances to practice personal poverty in small ways. When he has a chance to buy, for example, clothes, he can make a conscious effort to be truly economical—not necessarily by buying the cheapest, since they will soon wear out; nor by buying the most expensive, since they will last longer; but by keeping an eye open for bargains that will be thrifty and unostentatious; in other words, by doing just about what an involuntarily poor man would, plus the care to avoid the appearance of luxury. The same would apply to buying meals, equipment, books for study, entertainment and the like. Small, habitual gestures of poverty thus become not tokens but meaningful symbols.

Personal poverty will often require real courage in witnessing to others outside the religious life. For example, one must be able to tell parents no, when they suggest giving one expensive watches, transistor radios, clothes. He will not be too proud to beg from family or friends for works that need money—foreign missions, for example, or inner-city projects, or scholarships for indigent students. He can learn about the "feel" of poverty by doing some voluntary work with the poor. He will use public transportation rather than taxis (except in the case of emergencies or real need, such as a poor person would). He will avoid cultivating expensive or chic tastes in liquor or dining out. He will not make "the most of a good thing," even when the "good thing" is unsolicited.

No less important and pervasive is the kind of witness the religious can give in his use of time. Since time is money, he can and should make the most of it. Without lapsing into puritanism or scrupulosity, he should make sure that he doesn't become an "academic slob" while engaged in study. He can work hard to obtain scholarships or grants, as his less wealthy secular peers do. He can ration the time spent supinely before the TV set, or in passive reading. He can exercise mature choices in the matter of work, hobbies and rest.

Participation in Poverty

Community poverty can be greatly helped by a sense of participation. Community discussions will facilitate honesty in the mode of life. It may not be too much to say that the witness and reality of community poverty will vary in direct proportion to the openness of discussion on poverty at the community level. Communities that have access to budgets and spend time together studying them will hardly be extravagant. In smaller communities especially, such openness will promote a spirit of corporate poverty. Often unrealistic attitudes toward money are based on lack of information that could easily be available: the price of long-distance calls, drinks, the use of cars, medical services and the like.

The money saved by corporate poverty can be put to the service of the poor, either poorer communities, poor families, our own employees (who are sometimes paid less than justice calls for). In this regard the apostolic nature of religious poverty should be kept in mind. Thus savings might be agreed upon and diverted to specific apostolic projects.

It would be good if religious houses were situated in truly poor neighborhoods and reflected, not so much the mood of oases of security, as that of authentic sharing in the way of life of the poor. Living arrangements should show close identification with them. In any case, our facilities should not shield us from contact with the poor.

The real concern that young religious and many young diocesan priests feel about the material assets which tend to identify us with the upper-middle class or rich should not be lightly dismissed as youthful first fervor or quirkiness. I have known a young diocesan priest who refused the ordination present of an expensive car, because he felt that, even without a vow of poverty, he should be present among the poor as one of them. Young religious, too, are dismayed at any symbols of wealth shown by the community. They feel that expensive institutional structures—products of the "edifice complex"—are not only counter-witnesses but exercise a control over our own apostolic freedom. How many Catholic institutions, for example, have been hesitant about true racial integration or other Christian values out of fear of monetary loss? This troubles many a young religious or priest.

Race and Poverty

Thus it was that when Fr. Pedro Arrupe, superior general of the Society of Jesus, wrote his much publicized letter of November 1, 1967, on race and poverty, the younger Jesuits at large welcomed it enthusiastically. He pointed out bluntly that American Jesuits have shown a reluctance to "implement the fullness of Christian doctrine" in the matter of race, and that even at present "some of our institutions have effected what seems to be little more than token integration of the Negro."

He further suggested, among the reasons for our failure, "the insulation of far too many Jesuits [if you wish, read "religious and priests"] from the actual living conditions of the poor, and hence of most Negroes" and "an unarticulated fear of the reprisals sometimes visited on those who participate in the active Negro apostolate." As a corrective, he reminded all American Jesuits (and I suppose most other American religious might feel that they could say the same thing to themselves) that "our apostolate must be soundly predicated upon our personal and collective testimony to the real poverty of Christ," that "the needs of the world and the condition of the poor constitute a mandate and an incentive to remodel our own living standards."

Many religious, of course, of all ages do practice a dedication to the poor and share in their condition while working to improve it. But the question being asked on all sides, especially by the young, is whether our commitments have not become so institutionalized and gargantuan as to deprive us both of responsibility and of freedom. Accordingly, among suggestions sometimes offered (and the Santa Clara Conference included this specifically) is that religious be given opportunities for living and working among the poor; this might include taking laborers' jobs during the summer. The idea, like any new idea, is not without risks. But, as the founding fathers of any great religious-life tradition testify, risks are part of the stuff of holy initiatives.

XI
Program of
Formation

THIS CHAPTER will not do more than suggest a few basic concepts that seem to come up whenever seminary or religious-life academic training is discussed. As we go into specifics, the treatment will be of more applicability to one life, less to another. Thus, for example, religious brothers and sisters do not approach theology in quite the same way as do future priests. Nor do diocesan priests, as a rule, have a period of training in the novitiate. First, then, the most generalized norms.

Whether religious or priests are planning to dedicate their apostolic activity to education or not, it seems too evident for argument that they should achieve at least the level of education that Americans take for granted today. This means, roughly, the equivalent of a college degree. In the case of those who are not to be involved in teaching, nursing or social work, and who are presumed not to need a formal degree, they should have the opportunity to achieve the type of excellence needed to do their work well. We are not living in a class-conscious society; neither peasants nor proletarians are part of the American way of life. Thus, it is altogether unrealistic in America today—and the future will presumably find it no more realistic—for any group to be systematically treated as inferior.

No Class Society

Accordingly, any residual traces of "classes" or "grades" within a religious community should quickly disappear. Human dignity is not incompatible with humility. Humility should not be alleged as an excuse for depriving any religious of the development that measures up to his God-given capacity. Abnegation and mortification can be practiced with great intensity in the process of achieving an appropriate excellence in various skills. It does not need to be artificially imposed by keeping anyone "in his place." His true place should be one of dignity described in the whole of chapter 1 of Vatican II's *Constitution on the Church in the Modern World*. We cannot arbitrarily deny to any religious what the Council states in the *Decree on Christian Education;* namely, "Since every man of whatever race, condition and age is endowed with the dignity of a person, he has an inalienable right to an education corresponding to his proper destiny and suited to his native talents. . . ." It would be a source of genuine scandal if religious institutes, pledged to special service of the Church, were to disregard this unambiguous and solemn teaching of the Church.

Call for Education

Whatever the apostolic work envisaged, the course of studies for religious or priests should be given in terms of real life. Thus, it should be a thoroughly modern education, geared to the needs of the present time and to whatever we may reasonably project about the future. Further, it should continue throughout the individual's life. In our age of accelerating change, and with the continuing explosion of knowledge in every field, no sensible person can ever sit back in complacency as though his education were complete. Not merely is his general education endlessly open to growth; his specialty, too, must be constantly deepened and broadened. This applies no less to the techniques of grammar school teaching than to theology or nuclear physics. In any area of competence, to stop growing is to fossilize.

This means, not only that a religious or priest should never stop his program of self-education, reading periodicals and books in his field, but also that provision should be offered for him to take appropriate formal courses long after his terminal degree or certificate of skills. For we need to renew contacts with the academic or professional community in order not to grow stale, whether we are dieticians, counselors, engineers, theologians, catechists or high-school English teachers. Otherwise time passes us by and our service to God and God's people becomes outdated. As Etienne Gilson said so well, "Piety does not dispense with technique"; to be less excellent than our gifts warrant in the service of God is no compliment to him.

This implies, it need hardly be said, that in addition to a broad education everyone should achieve mastery (again proportionate to his gifts) in some area related to his broader vocation. In an era of specialization, we cannot afford not to be specialists. Priests are expected to be at least the equals of educated laity in theology.

Theology for All

Not that every priest can become a really specialized theologian; still less should he pretend to be one simply because he has gone through the standard or improved seminary course. But he should at least be *au courant* of the exciting movements in contemporary theology. Little doubt but that the troubling gap between educated laity in this country and very many of the clergy has been allowed to develop because many of the laity are much better read in modern theology than many priests. Today's young priests and seminarians should resolve mightily not to allow this lag to occur in their cases.

The need for theology among brothers and sisters will depend on their specific congregation's work. Whereas a few years ago it was rare to find highly trained theologians who were not priests, today we have a considerable number of theologians who are brothers and sisters, as well as laymen, and these are among our most distinguished. But even those brothers and sisters who are not planning to teach college theology are expected to be at least non-professional theologians.

Indeed, during their course of studies, from the novitiate on, they should become sufficiently competent to have reached a state of theological confidence, the ability to understand contemporary theological problems and to find solutions appropriate to their personal spiritual and intellectual needs. Further, they should become as competent as possible in those areas of theology that impinge on their specialty. And this not only for personal benefit but also for the help they will be expected to provide when dealing with their fellow professionals who are not religious but who reasonably expect religious to grasp the theological dimensions of their specialty. While this is especially the case with teachers, it also applies in varying degrees to those involved in other apostolates. A social worker, for example, will be expected to be well informed in the Church's social teaching.

Again, regardless of one's field of specialization, he should be at home in cultural anthropology, especially in an understanding of American culture and society. We take for granted that missionaries to foreign lands will study missiology—at least the amount of anthropology needed if one is to be effective in service there. While we are not so uninformed with regard to our own native culture, it would be useful to study it systematically. This not, of course, to make us chauvinistic in our American-ism, but to make us effective in serving our own people. Our Catholicity and the growing global consciousness of modern man make it also imperative that we gain some knowledge of cultures beyond our own, as well as a deep sensitivity to the international dimensions of modern life.

Danger of New Rigidity

It is important for us not to feel a false security based on the beginnings of changes already made. The real task is not simply that of an aggiornamentized curriculum, but the personal application of this curriculum to the individual and his talents and needs. Some seminaries that have already tried out a transitional curriculum seem to fall back into a rigidity that may be more dan-gerous that what it replaced. If the Spirit has urged us to recognize the signs of the times, the same Spirit has pressed us to be concerned for the individual, to recog-nize his uniqueness. Curriculum anxiety on the part of administrators and agenda anxiety on the part of teachers show a total misunderstanding of what *aggiornamento* is all about.

Now to the question of where seminaries and houses of religious formation should be situated. Everyone who has been "through the mill" can make a litany of advantages derived from a rather secluded location, where distractions were few and an atmosphere of quiet and study seemed to prevail. Accordingly, hackles may rise at the very suggestion that such a situation was not the best possible.

What appears to me a true consensus at present among students of the problem—at least, this comes through in most of the writing on the subject and at the seminars and conferences I have attended—is that, except for strict contemplatives, priests and religious should be educated in close proximity to real life. Seminaries should be situated in a college or university complex. Juniorates and the like should be either on or very near campuses, preferably coeducational campuses. Young seminarians and religious should have very much of their course work in connection with their peers in the secular world. They should learn to deal with them and compete with them and (as we have discussed in another chapter) have personal relationships with them. The less related to such real-life situations their formation is, the less likely it is to be effective for life.

Too Middle Class

Furthermore, they should not be sheltered from other aspects of reality. Most of our vocations in America come from middle-class families. Thus, whether or not the young people rebel against one or other middle-class value, they remain deeply conditioned by their early environment. If they are to escape from this and learn anything about the millions of poor Americans living not far from the campus, though commonly invisible there, they must have opportunities, on a regular basis, for social apostolates. This (as we discussed in the chapter on Poverty) will vary somewhat according to the academic set-up: some will find more time in summer, others can do more during the academic year, but at no university that I know is there no time for real social involvement with the poor and underpriviliged. If lay students and non-Christian students find time to serve the unfortunate, how much more evident is it that Christ's special followers should be able to find time to serve him in his least brethren.

It will, of course, require considerable discernment of spirits and dialogue with one's directors to balance this off with the serious pursuit of academic excellence, and not allow activism to serve as a pretext for evasion of what is one's main work for the time being. Even so, this is a risk worth taking, a risk that needs, in fact, to be taken.

New-Style Novitiate

Something should be said about the novitiate (and in this I am following rather closely the opinions of the novice directors who participated in the Santa Clara Conference and the final consensus papers of the Conference). The novice comes to the novitiate with his own spirituality, conditioned by the spirituality of the Church in the modern world. The novitiate should not be thought of as a withdrawal from this modern world. To be sure, an element of withdrawal is appropriate so that the novice may engage in serious reflection, both alone and in dialogue with his community. But the withdrawal must not be over-emphasized (as it usually has been in the recent past); still less must it be out of continuity with what the novice is preparing himself for.

Rather, the novitiate is a period in which the candidate is helped in his attempts to follow the Spirit in intensifying his whole life in the service of Christ in a particular community. This experience takes place in a living community, and not in a vacuum. It is a community in which novices and directors communicate with each other openly. Together they reflect upon their communal experience as they confront the world around them in the active apostolate of the particular institute. This experience will be deepened by an active confrontation with the word of God and by participation in a vibrant, developing liturgy. The novitiate will emphasize openness to the Spirit, and will be a continuing effort at spiritual discernment. Everything should be done to aid the novices and their directors to increase self-awareness, self-acceptance and social sensitivity in view of their service of God and God's people.

Novitiate for Real Life

The novitiate should continually define itself in terms of the apostolate of the particular institute, present and projected, toward which the novices' development is directed. The novitiate should emphasize its continuity with the rest of the life of the novices life both before and after the novitiate. Thus, the novitiate is not an end in itself. It should provide sufficient preparation for smooth transitions to later stages in the young religious' growth. Attitudes and practices should not be radically different as one passes from one stage to another. Otherwise what

has been acquired will quickly become irrelevant and the
novitiate will have been dysfunctional if not worthless.

Too often novices have been left with the impression
that the novitiate represents some sort of climax of spiritual development or a goal achieved, such that future
developments will always be judged according to life as
it was lived in the novitiate. The novitiate at its best
should impart a genuine understanding of the true spirit
of the founder and the best interpretation of the community's traditions. But this does not mean, nor should it
seem to mean, that the novitiate is a Golden Age precisely
normative for other circumstances, nor that it precludes
real growth in later life. The lived experience of these
norms may well mean departure from certain externals
that seemed to mark one's progress during the novitiate stage.

Hence, the novitiate should allow for serious academic and other work that will be continuous with what
will come later. Some of the novitiate training should be
taken in the "inner city" or other impoverished areas.
Novices should be given a chance to live in non-novi-
tiate houses, where they can discover what "the life" is
really like. This will help avoid crises later on; more
importantly, from such real experiences novices can
achieve a "feed-back" which will help their novitiate
work bear on the future.

Novitiates should welcome visiting members of the
institute; indeed, a wide variety of representative members should be invited to speak to the novices and participate in their on-going dialogue. Members of other
institutes and professional lay men and women should be
invited to do the same. Thus, qualified doctors, psychologists and other skilled persons should be called in to assist

in the novices' psychological instruction and development.

It should be too evident to need discussion that the novices' life of prayer ought to be a true initiation into the life of prayer that will be lived in later years. To break up the day into tiny fragmented parcels, ringing bells every few minutes, not allowing any time for consecutive work nor any discretionary time for individual initiative, is to create a sense that nothing really matters except automatic responses to arbitrary orders. This is not only injurious to personal growth in prayer and academic seriousness, but tends to demean obedience, the sense of responsibility and the finest resources of the developing person. Novices must learn through experience how to plan their day, allowing proportionate time for formal prayer, study, other work, service to others. Community prayer, especially the liturgy, must never seem something merely mechanical or done simply because it has always been done. Nor should it eliminate the need for privacy or personal flexibility.

The total separation of novices or other young religious from their families may have made sense in other times, but today it is unnatural and counterproductive. Apart from considerations of charity, most novices can profit greatly from contacts with their family, both in visits from them and, occasionally at least, by visiting their homes. Such visits help both in appreciation of their personal background and self-understanding, and in deglamorizing unreal nostalgic memories. Somewhat the same may be said with regard to visits from one's former classmates and old friends.

Renewal Programs

Most religious communities make some provision for

a "second novitiate" or "tertianship" after the course of studies and after some years of service. The enormous advantages that can derive from this experience are beyond cavil. Nor, I suppose, would anyone favor dropping this tradition. What very often needs change is a certain rigidity as regards the length of time for the second novitiate and the scheduling. For not everyone needs it at the same moment of life, nor does he need exactly a fixed number of months. Still less need it be identical in structure for every person or group. The objectives should be clearly identified; then steps taken to eliminate everything that does not serve the objectives, and to add whatever is needed. Among these objectives, as I see them, would be: developing a deeper sense of community, a fuller understanding of the oral tradition of one's religious institute, a reevaluation of one's personal development, a reassessment of the community's apostolates and one's part in them.

In addition to the second novitiate or tertianship, it would be very advisable to have an occasional program of renewal for older religious who desire it. The program would, of course, be most flexible, stressing the needs of the older religious and allowing them time for reflection, for scriptural studies, for lectures and seminars on developments in current theology. Such an investment of time by the community will surely be repaid in increased enthusiasm and flexibility among the older members. It would also help deepen the realization that one's development, both intellectual and spiritual, is a never-ending process.

The formation program, then, must be adjusted to the needs of the person who will engage in the apostolic work of community or diocese. It must be treated with vast flexibility and geared to the development of persons not personnel. It must never be so fixed as to become ill adapted to the changing needs of the Church, and thus ineffectual. Even the newest structures must not be thought of as set, but must be continually adapted to the individuals and their needs. For this, we need constant, on-going discernment of what the Spirit is telling us at each moment. Such discernment, finally, is the work of no single person, but of the community of persons.

XII
Dreams and
Visions

THIS FINAL chapter can hardly be a recapitulation of what is already a tight recapitulation of many group experiences. Instead it will offer a few reflections on several concerns that have been left untouched previously or at best touched only lightly. The title alludes, of course, to Peter's sermon in *Acts*, where he quotes the prophet Joel: "Your young men shall see visions and your old men shall dream dreams." For this is one of the clearest scriptural hints at the change and continuity that go to make up life and the life of the Church. Visions are often of the future; dreams, often of the past: *change and continuity*.

Age and youth have their preferred axioms: "nothing succeeds like success" or "nothing ventured nothing gained." Each is quick to find the inadequacy or partiality of the other's slogans. A convenient riposte to one is "nothing fails like success" (witness the Maginot Line fiasco, based on the trench formula that worked well a generation earlier), and to the other, "nothing ventured nothing lost."

Tempting as it is to believe, it is not true (as some elders seem to hold) that "all we have in common is our past"; nor is it true (as some younger people seem to hold) that "all we have in common is the future." What we have in common is, really, both past and future, linked in the precarious present. However obvious this platitude is, often it is overlooked, as competing attitudes push only one way. We need both the dreamers and the seers, and we need their shared perceptions.

Leadership

If we may base our projections on the past, at least to some extent, we have reason to believe that today's young religious and seminarians will be expected to play a leadership role. Again and again—and not only in the remote past—men and women of God have been leaders, in thought, action, vision. Many of these have been religious or priests; one thinks immediately of such varied giants as Benedict, Aquinas, Francis, Vincent de Paul, Newman, Teilhard and those in our time who inspired Vatican II. The future, doubtless, will see a healthy increase in lay leadership, and it is not clear what precise tasks Providence has for religious and priests, say, in the 21st or 22nd centuries. History, however, suggests that the tasks will be similar; that is to say, some will be the same (witnessing selflessly to Christ) and some will be different, and unforeseeable (as they have always been unforeseeable in the past). But leadership, in one form or another, will have to be exercized.

A leader is someone who motivates others and who encourages them and generates enthusiasm and keeps an eye on the future. He has a keen sense of "goals." He has vision of where we ought to be going (related to faith), the capacity to encourage people to get there (hope), and the capacity to motivate people to reach out toward these goals (love).

Viewed this way (as it was during the Santa Clara Conference), leadership is not a fearsome thing, a dread consequence of pride and the fall, something not to soil our hands on. It is charismatic, hence good. At the same time, it is elusive. Leadership is a relationship between persons and situations; accordingly, no one type of preparation is appropriate for all. Yet, if priests and religious are to prepare themselves for leadership situations, three ingredients of preparation must be present: a climate in which leadership is valued, opportunities for the exercise of leadership, programs in which appropriate knowledge can be acquired.

Fr. Bernard Cooke has suggested a brief outline for a theology of leadership under the three headings mentioned above: faith, hope, love. Faith is more than an intellectual assent; it is the acceptance of the challenge which comes in the personal order from Christ himself. Further, the process of revelation shows that faith really grows in response to concrete life situations, and that the prophetic voice is one of "understanding the present with its challenges in the light of the tradition of faith which has come to us from the past." Hope adds to encouragement a new dimension, by which men are encouraged to strive after goals difficult of attainment.

Further, if there is going to be leadership that will be truly Christian (and this, above all, should be our motivation for working toward leadership), it must be guided by theological clarity and depth. It is sometimes appalling to see decisions made, even after Vatican II, "in almost total abstraction from, if not denial of, what contemporary theology would tell us about the nature and mission of the Church." One thinks of the token gestures toward *aggiornamento* that really block the type of reform urgently needed.

What happened at Vatican II indicates something else that we must pay attention to: "It is the recognition of the fact that the Church has, rather slowly but now rather definitively, been touched by what is happening in contemporary society . . . that we have moved out of a feudal approach to leadership into a situation of leadership that would be called dialogic . . . its insistence on the fact that all the baptized share the mission of Christ." Thus, leadership is not confined to those in official positions.

Further, in the new context of leadership (not as power but as service), we who belong to orders that do not elect their local superiors should "perhaps have more to say about who our leaders will be, and that having had more of a voice in who their leaders will be, we will identify with them more consistently and continue to act with them in the process of their exercise and leadership" (to quote Fr. Cooke again).

Service of the World

Our dedication to the vision of Vatican II should open us, as persons pledged to special service of the Church, to what Vatican II calls for today and in the immediate future. Among these special summonses of the Council, in the *Constitution on the Church in the Modern World,* are surely: that we work toward international dialogue and respect and love for all men (n. 28); that we help the world to overcome all forms of prejudice dividing mankind (n. 29); that we promote interpersonal union and a "wholesome socialization" among men (n. 42); that we help build a better world based upon truth and justice (n. 55); that we work to foster peace and the community of nations (nn. 63-93). In this country especially, as we have seen in the chapter on poverty, religious and priests will surely take a serious part in helping to bring about racial justice and equality. To do otherwise would be to become accomplices in our greatest national crime.

The fact that our witness stresses the "vertical," the eschatological aspect of the Incarnation, and that much of the tradition of religious life in the past has focused on renunciation rather than acceptance of certain human values, cannot blind us to the Church's new involvement in the world. True, different approaches to the religious life have their special meaning and are part of the total Christian inheritance. No one should want to see diversity disappear.

Yet there is a certain general tonality to Catholicism in this late 20th century, and Vatican II enunciates it variously and frequently. Its desire was, explicitly, "to speak to all men in order to illuminate the mystery of man and to cooperate in finding the solution to the outstanding problems of our time" (*Church in the Modern World*, n. 10). All of us, lay, religious and priest—even if our special vocation is one of extreme austerity and detachment—must be fully concerned about the best values of humanity, the humanity which Christ redeemed.

Dialogue with Atheists

The image of Christianity as unconcerned, as an anti-humanism, has been the main anti-religious impulse among Marxists and other secular humanists. Teilhard de Chardin cautioned us Christians that "a religion judged to be inferior to our human ideal is a lost religion." For if we give the appearance of not being involved, of judging human institutions too unimportant to merit our concern, we inescapably seem allied with the powers that want things as they are: with the destitution of most of mankind to the advantage of the few. In this sense not only Marxists but other atheistic humanists despise or even hate religion as "the opiate of the people."

Vatican II, however, offered little comfort to those who favored the socio-economic *status quo.* Nor did Pope John's *Pacem in Terris* or Pope Paul's *Populorum Progressio,* with their forward thrust in the Church's social teaching. Neither of these encyclicals was much praised in bourgeois Catholic milieux: they called for the abandonment of chauvinistic attitudes, and brought out once again that the role of Christianity is not that of a bulwark for the rich—in this case, the rich and powerful nations —against others. I found it heartening, in fact, to hear Roger Garaudy, a leading Marxist theoretician, admit that after the Council and Popes John and Paul, he thought Marx would detect little of the smell of opium in Catholicism. I also thought, with some regret, that many churchmen and religious are still doing little to dispel that odor, preferring the attitudes of those who don't want change in the world.

Religious, I believe, should be more able than others to enter into dialogue with atheistic humanists, Marxist or otherwise. For with their witness of poverty, if it is authentic, they are certainly liberated from ultra-capitalist or ultra-conservative viewpoints, at least as regards wealth. Their poverty becomes not anti-humanistic but more deeply participative in the broad human condition. Without self-attachment they can work more truly for a truly human society. "The achievement of a truly human society," Robert A. Johann says, "is a task for man himself." To be religious, whether in the lay state or otherwise, should mean that one loves man, since he cannot love God without loving man; and to love man without laboring to improve man's condition is a mockery of love.

To be a Christian—and this must be mostly the case with those specially pledged to living their baptism to the full—means to idolize neither the past nor the present, since our Lord is the eschatological Lord, to whom we unceasingly pray: "Come, Lord Jesus!" During a recent Marxist-Catholic dialogue, Karl Rahner defined Christianity as "the religion of the absolute future." This does not mean that we can be casual about the immediate future, basking in utopian dreams; for part of the task is always immediately ahead. But it does mean that we must keep our sights from falling too low, by failing to work for the farther kingdom, both before and after the resurrection. The only answer to atheistic humanism and the only contribution we can make to the Christian-humanist dialogue is a developing Christian humanism. This is something that every religious and priest can make a serious contribution to, whether his work is in school, parish, hospital, slum or foreign mission.

Internationalism

To be a Catholic is to be internationally oriented. Religious and priests, by their full-time service, are expected to be open to other nations, other cultures, other worlds. Vatican II opened with a cordial message to all men and nations, expressing concern for "the hardships, the bodily and mental distress, the sorrows, longings, and hopes of all peoples" and pledging its dedication to "whatever concerns the dignity of man, whatever contributes to a genuine community of peoples." The Council described itself in its very diversity of nations and races as "a witness to the community of brotherly love and a visible sign . . . that all men are brothers, whatever their race or nation." (*Opening Message to Humanity*) Freed from many confining obligations in order to be more open to broader service, religious and priests should think, pray, feel and, as far as humanly possible, personally serve beyond parochial limits.

Those religious who belong to international congregations and orders have a special opportunity to be more "catholic" in their service. It would make very good sense if, instead of merely fulfilling modern language requirements in pursuit of a college degree, they took every chance to speak a second language. History, psychology, sociology, anthropology can, if treated seriously, help to make a student internationally minded. Religious have unusual opportunities to do some study abroad, and while abroad to live not as an enclave of exiled Americans, but as citizens of the world. An unexpected by-product of internationalism is, as anyone who has lived abroad must know, a deepened understanding of one's own culture. Only by discovering differences can one grasp what he personally is.

It would be healthy, too, if superiors gave as many religious as possible a chance to do "junior year abroad"; often such an investment is slight in terms of money, but brings incalculable returns. Many colleges and universities offer inexpensive summer sessions in Mexico or other countries. Such experiences, which require more effort than money, can prove far more than recreational or merely broadening in a vague sort of way. Exchange programs between religious houses or other institutions can go a long way toward eliminating mental barriers between nations.

Today all sorts of service opportunities are open to religious and seminarians. PAVLA, VISTA, CIASP and other projects aimed at helping the poor should not be the exclusive privilege of lay students. It is not necessary to make a lifetime commitment to them in order to do real good or to gain considerable enlightenment in an international way.

Missions

We belong to a missionary Church. Indeed, missionary work is the fulfillment of God's will in the world and world history, as Vatican II pointed out (*Decree on Missions*, n. 9). Like Christ, we as Catholics should enter into truly human conversation with all men (n. 11) and should learn to "identify" with other cultures (n. 19). If in the past the Church has been overly identified with cultures that derive from Europe, this is understandable and to an extent excusable in terms of history. Today, however, for the first time, the Church has the physical means to become universal and catholic. Communications and international structures make it possible for men really to meet. In the long view, this can be seen as providentially inspired, part of God's plan "that the whole body of men which makes up the human race should form one People of God" (*Decree on Missions*).

The American Church has, in recent years, begun to play its part in the missions, even though it still lags far behind such other countries as Holland and Spain. Some of the problem is the American over-commitment of most religious orders, on whom missionary activity has thus far fallen. True, we have several societies founded in this country, like the Maryknoll fathers and sisters, for work abroad; and we have groups who stress much needed home missions, especially among Negroes and the under-privileged. Further, several dioceses have sent volunteer priests and seminarians to Latin America.

But those religious communities dedicated to the active life should, as the Council solemnly requests (*Decree on Missions*, n. 40), "sincerely ask themselves in the presence of God, whether they cannot broaden their activity in favor of expanding God's kingdom among the nations; whether they might not leave certain ministries to others so that they themselves can spend their energies on the missions; whether they can undertake work among the missions, *adapting their constitutions if necessary*, but according to the spirit of their founder; whether their members are involved as much as possible in missionary activity; and whether their type of life bears to the gospel a witness adapted to the character and condition of the people." Be it noted, further, that this series of concrete requests is adapted to congregations "whether they pursue a strictly mission goal or not."

Ecumenism

Another area of vision, where the future is ever so much brighter than the past, is that of ecumenism and inter-faith understanding. More and more, especially in this country, priests and religious are involved in discourse with non-Catholics, and in fact with non-Christians. Especially those priests, sisters and brothers who are skilled in theology have a growing role in this important dialogue. While the early initiatives along ecumenical lines occurred in Europe, and for years America was far behind, it seems that the initiative has now passed, in great part, to our country. It may even be that the future of Christian reunion depends very largely upon what is accomplished here.

Since much ecumenical activity will be carried on at the scholarly level, it is important that a number of theologically competent people get professional preparation for the work of theological discourse with non-Catholics, and for the help of the laity in ecumenical work. They need to learn about other faiths by study, by reading and by personal contact. They need, especially, to learn their faith in the pluralistic context, where sympathetic comparison and contrast are a great help. It would be good, since no one can be a universal specialist, to become especially conversant with at least one particular religious position beyond Catholicism.

Much of this can, of course, be achieved through direct ecumenical or inter-faith dialogue, as they learn to deal with others personally and at complete ease. Dialogue between seminarians from Catholic and other divinity schools should be a normal element in theological education. It is obvious, too, that cooperative efforts on social questions and theological research on an institutional level between Catholic and non-Catholic divinity schools should be increased.

It should not be supposed that ecumenical attitudes are the preserve of the trained few. Each has a part in the larger task, at least in terms of love, sympathy and the abandonment of the tribalism that makes us want to be separate and superior. Even without being expert theologians, all religious and priests can and should make an effort to understand what contemporary theology is really about, and not be satisfied to repeat new slogans.

If one's bent is ultra-conservative, he can at least attend lectures or launch into a program of systematic reading designed at understanding what people like Rahner, Congar, Schillebeeckx, Metz, de Lubac and others are contributing. What Fr. Avery Dulles calls "the dangers of non-historical orthodoxy and clerical paternalism" should be candidly faced; for not everything that passes for orthodoxy is really rooted in history, nor is the clerical to be identified with the Catholic. Hard as it may be to admit, our old anti-Protestantism was rooted more in tribalism than in Christianity. Religious have a special opportunity, in their very commitment and the freedom it offers, to escape tribalistic traps. For, of all the people of God, they should be among the least shackled by attachments to the past, and the readiest to live by hope.

The real threat to religious life and the priesthood today is, I believe, not so much the radicalism of the young or the immobility of many of their elders. It is, rather, disillusionment, timidity, fear—in short, a failure of hope. The occasional article or book censoriously attacking the Church for being outmoded fails less in what it says than in what it omits. If one looks only forward at what is undone, then one may see things cynically, dyspeptically, humorlessly. It is much like the amateur mountain climber, who as he moves up the slope finds his progress slower and drabber. The mountain loses its glamor, seen from too close. The pull it once exerted gets weaker. Each step upward seems unrewarding. Only when one looks back—not in the Gospel sense of turning away from the plow—does one sense progress and process. Only then are tremendous vistas opened up. One cannot only trudge along; one must stop occasionally to receive the vision afforded. As William Ernest Hocking puts it, we must alternate between worship and work, between being mystic and prophet. Today there is real need for prophets; the prophetical role is much esteemed. But to be true prophets we must be mystics, seers. The only true vision is the whole vision.

Just as this book was being finished, a group of priest-religious friends presented me with a statement drawn up by them at the conclusion of their recent retreat. As old companions who had been through novitiate and seminary together, and then gone into varied apostolates, they came together again to share and reflect on their diversified personal experiences: theologians, philosophers, pastors, retreat masters, teachers, writers, artists. Every thought and word of their statement was carefully meditated on and prayed over, and it seems to express so perfectly the themes underpinning the present volume that I am delighted to print it here. Only the name of the religious order is omitted, since its application, I believe, extends wider than any single religious institute.

"We believe that what binds us together as a community is in the first instance our commitment to Christ and our friendship and love for one another in his name; second, our belief that our order is capable of a genuine renewal of spirit and of as radical a reshaping of its apostolic structures as may be required so that it may function in fact as well as in aspiration as a fit instrument of God in a thoroughly contemporary Church;

third, our commitment to our order's principle of greater
service: that we can allow no attachment to past accom-
plishments and structures to deter us from the pursuit of
what seems to us in conscience to be for the greater
praise and service of God.

"We believe that as members of our order we have
been called by God to serve Christ not merely as individuals but as members of an apostolic community and
that according to the mind of our founder our specific
raison d'être as a community consists in our readiness to
respond with constant flexibility to whatever may be the
greatest apostolic needs of the moment.

"Therefore, we believe that the time has come for us
to begin to question concretely and with blunt honesty
to ourselves and before God whether the specific apostolic commitments in which we are currently engaged
are truly allowing us to serve God and his Church with
the effectiveness, deep personal dedication, and peace of
soul which Christ demands of us. We do not believe that
there is any option concerning the need for this reassessment or any *a priori* limits that can be placed on its
consequences. The Pope and all the bishops in Council
together with our own superior general and our general
congregation demanded it of us; and if we are to be true
sons of the Church and of our order, we must obey. We
therefore believe that this reassessment is not only a
practical necessity but even a necessity of faith, and that
resistance to such a mandate will only prolong the con-
flicts and divisions in our communities.

"We also believe that the work of reassessment must
be in every sense of the term a community endeavor
which will demand of each of us the willingness to make
every possible concession to viewpoints other than our

own. We believe that each member of our order must be willing to face the fact that there is much needless suffering in many of our communities as a result of our common refusal to face the hard realities of the situations in which we live and work and as a result of our constant human tendency to substitute in our imaginations the ideal that we would like to be for the imperfect human reality that we are.

"Finally, we cannot at the present time see how community can be achieved until there is a firm commitment on the part of each of us to the following principles:

"1. That we must first genuinely be concerned to discover the meaning of another's statement before we become concerned with either its authority or its truth; and that we must be willing to take whatever time is necessary to discover that meaning;

"2. That the truth of any situation is more important than the established position or opinion of any individual or of any institution;

"3. That we must speak the truth with love, valuing a real community founded on truth and not the mere appearance of one; and that we must constantly reaffirm the fact that to disagree with another does not mean we hate him any more than to love another means we must agree with him;

"4. That our community exists for an apostolic purpose as well as for our mutual love and support; and that the effectiveness of our apostolate depends in direct proportion upon the love and happiness we foster within our communities;

"5. That institutional needs must never reduce us to using our own men as mere means in disregard of their personal needs; and that personal timidity and fear of speaking the truth must never prevent us from protesting such an abuse;

"6. That we must possess a real desire to worship together as a community, especially in the Eucharist; and that this desire should actually manifest itself in practice;

"7. That we must be willing to give to our superiors all the help, support and sympathy we can in the difficult work of renewal;

"8. That the achievement of the kind of community enunciated in these principles *is possible;* but

"9. That the achievement of community requires continual effort as well as leisure for the sharing in depth of our common experiences and ideals; and that the pace at which many of our institutions are presently run renders this impossible.

"Moreover, we believe that without these principles we can be faithful neither to the inspiration which motivated our founder in founding our order nor to the clear mandate of Vatican II and our own general congregation."

It would be hard, I submit, to find a more incisive, perceptive and Christian formulation of the work that should be immediately ahead of us.

Bibliographical
Suggestions

The following books and articles are recommended to spiritual directors who may want some further development of certain topics treated in the book. They in no sense represent a complete bibliography of spiritual direction. It is presupposed that the classic works are already available. These are only more recent items that might otherwise be missed. Two journals that should be in the hands of spiritual directors are REVIEW FOR RELIGIOUS (539 North Grand Blvd., St. Louis, Missouri 63103) and THE WAY (114 Mount St., London, W-1).

GENERAL ITEMS

A New Catechism: Catholic Faith for Adults (Herder & Herder. 1967), sections on priesthood pp. 357-371, and on religious life pp. 410-417

Magda B. Arnold and John A. Gasson, S.J., *The Human Person* (Ronald Press. 1954)

August Brunner, S.J., *A New Creation: Towards a Theology of the Christian Life* (Burns & Oates. 1955)

Paul F. D'Arcy, M.M., and Eugene C. Kennedy, M.M., *The Genius of the Apostolate* (Sheed & Ward. 1965)

John J. Evoy, S.J., and Van F. Christoph, S.J., *Maturity in the Religious Life* (Sheed & Ward. 1965)

John J. Evoy, S.J., and Van F. Christoph, S.J., *Personality Development in the Religious Life* (Sheed & Ward. 1963)

John J. Evoy, S.J., and Van F. Christoph, S.J., *The Real Woman in the Religious Life* (Sheed and Ward. 1967)

Viktor Frankl, *Man's Search for Meaning* (Washington Square Press. 1963)

Erich Fromm, *The Art of Loving* (Harper & Row. 1965) and paperback

Robert G. Gassert, S.J., and Bernard H. Hall, *Psychiatry and Religious Faith* (Viking Press. 1964)

Donald L. Gelpi, S.J., *Functional Asceticism: A Guideline for American Religious* (Sheed & Ward. 1966)

Josef Goldbrunner, *Realization: The Anthropology of Pastoral Care* (Notre Dame Press. 1966)

Reuel L. Howe, *The Miracle of Dialogue* (Seabury Press. 1963)

Eugene C. Kennedy, M.M., *Fashion Me a People: Man, Woman and the Church* (Sheed & Ward. 1967)

J. M. Lee and L. J. Putz, C.S.C., editors, *Seminary Education in a Time of Change* (Fides, 1965)

Barry McLaughlin, *Nature, Grace and Religious Development* (Newman. 1965)

Edwin M. McMahon, S.J., and Peter A. Campbell, S.J., *Becoming a Person in the Whole Christ* (Sheed and Ward. 1967)

Louis Monden, S.J., *Sin, Liberty and Law* (Sheed & Ward. 1965)

Joseph Nuttin, *Psychoanalysis and Personality: A Dynamic Theory of Normal Personality* (Mentor-Omega. 1962)

Hugh P. O'Neill, S.J., *The Concept of Personal Value* (University of Detroit Press. 1966)

Gerard S. Sloyan, editor *Secular Priest in the New Church* (Herder & Herder. 1967)

Paul Tournier, *The Meaning of Persons* (Harper & Row. 1957) ; *The Whole Person in a Broken World* (Harper & Row. 1964)

Adrian Van Kaam, C.S.Sp., *The Art of Existential Counseling* (Dimension Books. 1966)

Adrian Van Kaam, C.S.Sp., *Personality Fulfillment in the Religious Life*, vol. 1 (Dimension. 1967)

Adrian Van Kaam, C.S.Sp., *Religion and Personality* (Prentice-Hall. 1964)

COMMITMENT

Paul J. Bernadicou, S.J., "Persons and the Religious Life," in *Review for Religious* 23 (1964) pp. 596-603

Eugene Bianchi, S.J., "Religious Life and the Paschal Mystery," *Review for Religious* 23 (March 1964), pp. 174-184

Felix F. Cardegna, S.J., "Perfect Chastity and Human Affectivity," in *Review for Religious* 23 (1964) pp. 309-315

Felix F. Cardegna, S.J., "Religious Celibacy" in *The Sacred Heart Messenger* (March, 1967)

Jean Daniélou, S.J., "The Place of Religious in the Structure of the Church," in *Review for Religious* 24 (1965) pp. 518-525

Jean Galot, S.J., "Why Religious Life?" in *Review for Religious* 24 (1965) pp. 505-517

R. W. Gleason, S.J., "The Value of Virginity" in *To Live Is Christ*, pp. 117-134

Bernard Haering, C.Ss.R., "The Meaning of Celibacy," in *Pastoral Life* 14 (1966) pp. 5-9

Eugene Kennedy, M.M., "The Male Mystique," in *Critic* 24 (1966) pp. 26-31

L. Legrand, "Celibacy: Death and Sacrifice" in *Theology Digest* 11 (1963) pp. 114-118

Marc Oraison, *The Celibate Condition and Sex.* (Sheed and Ward. 1967)

Marc Oraison, *The Human Mystery of Sexuality* (Sheed and Ward. 1967)

Karl Rahner, S.J., "The Life of the Counsels," in *Theology Digest* 14 (1966) pp. 224-227

Herbert F. Smith, S.J., "Temporary Religious Vocation" in *Review for Religious* 23 (1964) pp. 433-444

Hans Urs von Balthasar, "A Theology of the Evangelical Counsels," in *Cross Currents* 16 (1966) pp. 213-236 and pp. 325-337

Friedrich Wulf, "Celibacy and Virginity," in *Theology Digest* 13 (1965), pp. 107-111

AUTHORITY AND OBEDIENCE

Lorenzo Boisvert, O.F.M., "The Nature of Religious Authority" in *Review for Religious* 24 (1965) pp. 34-54

August Brunner, S.J., "Religious Obedience Today" in *Theology Digest* 14 (1966) pp. 107-110

Thomas Corbishley, S.J., "Power and Authority," in *The Way* 3 (1963) pp. 285-293

Thomas Dubay, S.M., "Personal Integrity and Intellectual Obedience," in *Review for Religious* 22 (1963) pp. 493-501

Augustine G. Ellard, S.J., "A Rational Approach to Intellectual Obedience," in *Review for Religious* 14 (1955) pp. 261-265

Piet Fransen, S.J., "Grace and Freedom" in *Homiletic and Pastoral Review* 65 (1965), pp. 731-754

Robert O. Johann, S.J., "Authority and Fellowship" in *America* (April 23, 1966)

Robert O. Johann, S.J., "Authority and Responsibility" in *Catholic Mind* 63 (1965)

John L. McKenzie, S.J., *Authority in the Church* (Sheed and Ward. 1966)

John Courtney Murray, S.J., "Freedom, Authority, Community" in *America* (Dec. 3, 1966)

John Courtney Murray, S.J., "The Declaration on Religious Freedom: Its Deeper Significance" in *America* (April 23, 1966)

Kevin D. O'Rourke, O.P., "Obedience and Subsidiarity in Religious Life" in *Review for Religious* 25 (1966) pp. 305-313

Arturo Paoli, "Obedience" in *Cross Currents* 16 (1965) pp. 275-294

Karl Rahner, S.J., "A Basic Ignatian Concept: Some Reflections on Obedience," in *Cross Currents* 10 (1960) pp. 336-341

Joseph Ratzinger, S.J., "Frank Witness and Docile Obedience" in *Theology Digest* (Summer, 1965) 13:2

F. Joseph Smith, "The Demands of Honesty" in *Continuum* 2 (1964) pp. 210-219

POVERTY

William M. Barbieri, S.J., "The Young Religious and His

Poverty" in *Review for Religious* 25 (1966), pp.
288-293

Jean Danielou, S.J., "Evangelical Poverty" in *Theology
Digest* 11 (1963) pp. 57-59

Karl Rahner, S.J., "Religious Poverty in a Changing
World," in *Theology Digest* 11 (1963) pp. 49-56

PRAYER

Felix F. Cardegna, S.J., "Prayer in Religious Life" in
The Sacred Heart Messenger (April. 1967)

Joseph F. Conwell, S.J., *Contemplation in Action.* (Gon-
zaga University Press. 1957)

Jean Daniélou, S.J., *Prayer As a Political Problem*
(Sheed and Ward. 1967)

Leopold Malevez, S.J., "Liturgy and Private Prayer," in
Theology Digest 12 (1964) pp. 178-183

Mental Prayer and Modern Life: A Symposium especially essays by P. Philippe, O.P. and Robert Rou-
quette, S.J. (P. J. Kenedy, 1950)

William H. Quiery, S.J., *Facing God* (Sheed and Ward.
1967)

Karl Rahner, S.J., *Encounters With Silence* (Newman.
1965)

Emile Rideau, "Theology of Leisure," in *Theology
Digest* (Autumn, 1964) 12:3

Robert J. Roth, S.J., "Contemplation in Action," in
Review for Religious 21 (1962) pp. 531-540.

Paul Tournier, editor, *Fatigue in Modern Theology* (John
Knox Press. 1965)

COMMUNITY

Thomas Barrosse, C.S.C., "Religious Community and

the Primitive Church," in *Review for Religious* 25 (1966) pp. 971-985

Edward F. Heenan, S.J., "A Quest for Religious Community" in *Woodstock Letters* (Summer. 1967)

Francis X. Shea, S.J., "Small Communities in the Society of Jesus" in *Woodstock Letters* (Summer. 1967)

Hilary Smith, O.C.D., "The Family Fallacy," *Review for Religious* 25 (1966) pp. 1000-1017

Joseph H. Fichter, S.J., *Religion as an Occupation* (University of Notre Dame Press. 1961)